JUDITH COMFORT'S
CHRISTMAS
COOKBOOK

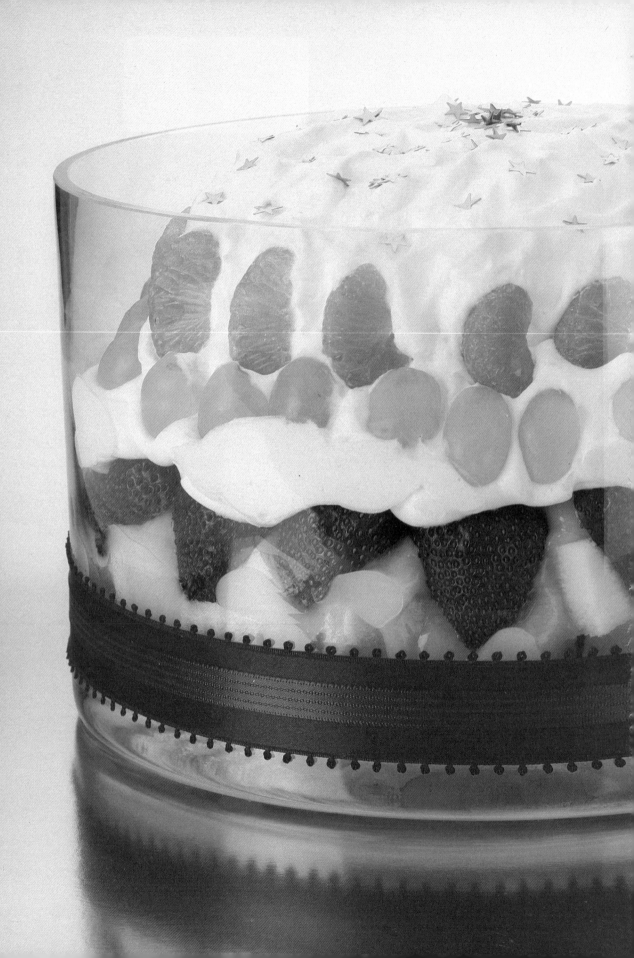

JUDITH COMFORT'S CHRISTMAS COOKBOOK

A Guide to Holiday Cooking and Entertaining

DOUBLEDAY CANADA LIMITED
TORONTO

Canadian Cataloguing in Publication Data

Comfort, Judith
  Judith Comfort's Christmas cookbook

ISBN 0-385-25155-6

1. Christmas cookery. I. Title. II. Title: Christmas cookbook.

TX739.C65 1988   641.5'68   C88-094523-0

Creative director and designer:
Catherine Wilson/C.P. Wilson Graphic Communication
Photography: Hal Roth Photography Inc.
  Assistant: Bill Hawkey

Food styling: C. Lee Crawford
  Rosemarie Superville
Props: Wally Suderman
  Special thanks to Liz Christie Antiques, Donna Coopman
  Brown, Maggie Reeves, Phyllis Black, Birks Jewellers, and
  St. Lawrence ChristmasMarket.

Production editor: Maggie Reeves
Editor: C. Lee Crawford

Typesetting: Southam Communications Limited

Printed and bound in Canada by
Friesen Printers Limited

Published by
Doubleday Canada Limited
105 Bond Street
Toronto, Ontario

Title page photograph:
English Trifle
(see recipe on page 176)

Front cover photograph:
My Favorite Plum Pudding
(see recipe on page 5)
Food stylist: Jennifer McLagan
Creative direction: Phyllis Black

Illustrations are from the books "Food and Drink: A Pictorial Archive from Nineteenth-Century Sources" and "An Old-Fashioned Christmas in Illustration & Decoration", published by Dover Publications, Inc., New York.

For Molly

CONTENTS

ACKNOWLEDGMENTS

I would like to thank all the friends and friends of friends who shared with me their Christmas memories and recipes: Molly Titus, Claire Titus, Mary and Herbert Puxley, Charlotte Reed, Linda Jane Mueller, Eric and Mary Holden, Jackie Welland, Martine Vermuelen, Gilli Holme, Mary Lucia Blacksher, Alice Trillin, Betty Seinen, Leni Seinen, Fran Whitelaw, Thomasine Boni, Kathy Chute, Phyllis Emerson, Margo Kleiker, Wendy Elliott, Anne Crosby, Zoya Coodin, Carlotta Smith, Vitalia Dibrosky Letson, Marie Kleiker Moes, Peggy Airey, Dianna Bowers, Isolde Savage, and Phillipa Campsie. Special thanks to Alan Comfort, my in-house grinch, to Maggie Reeves for pulling it all together and to Lee Crawford for her spirited overview.

*C*hristmas comes but once a year, but my family and I just spent a whole year celebrating Christmas while I put together this book. We nibbled on fruitcake in October and feasted on roast goose in November. We built a gingerbread house in January and made marzipan pigs in February. We drank eggnog whenever we felt like it and best of all, the children had cookies in their lunch boxes all year round. I realized all my Christmas food fantasies. I mixed up the homemade liqueurs that I had always wanted to try and experimented with twenty different turkey stuffings. And I talked Christmas all year, too. I was curious to find out what it is about this holiday that fills our imaginations for two full months, every year. I interviewed an 80-year-old Italian grandmother who vividly remembers playing bingo with her cousins after Christmas dinner and using orange peels to cover her numbers. Another friend who grew up on the banks of the St. Lawrence River remembers being awakened Christmas Eve to the wondrous sight of a tinsel-covered tree and the fragrance of her mother's tourtière pies. One cool summer evening I had the privilege of sharing Christmas past, spanning decades and continents, with a grandmother, her daughter and her granddaughter, while they reminisced about this special time of year. It was an exceptional year for me and I was grateful for the opportunity to research and record such a rich legacy.

Judith Comfort
Port Medway, Nova Scotia

MEATLESS MINCEMEAT
(see pages 26-27)

CHAPTER 1

GETTING
IN THE MOOD

ADVANCE BAKING

Christmas begins in November at our house. It starts the day I take down the large ceramic bowl from the top shelf and fill it with cherries, raisins, currants, molasses, buttermilk, rum, vanilla, allspice and cinnamon. The fruity incense of these blended ingredients defies description, but it is called plum pudding. ▰ The season begins for my neighbor when she takes her first batch of shortbread out of the oven. The butter-nut fragrance fills her house as she rolls the cookies in snowy icing sugar. ▰ Another friend sets aside two days in early November to make fruitcakes with her children. The first day they chop candied lemon and orange peel, citron and pecans and sift together the spices and flour. The second day they press the moist, fruit-studded batter into pans. As the loaves bake, the house fills with a spicy aroma which her children will forever associate with Christmas. Although the family does not taste a bite of cake until Christmas day, they have shared a relaxed time together and have been given the gift of expectation. ▰ For most of the year, our modern baking methods

— quick breads, instant yeast, microwave cakes and non-cook pudding mixes — emphasize instant gratification. But traditional Christmas foods — steamed puddings, fruitcakes, honey cookies and mincemeat — take patience and time to allow their special flavors to mellow. ※ Because Christmas cooking evolved long before modern refrigeration, traditional recipes seldom call for fresh ingredients. By December, when grapes were gone from the vine, dried raisins were savored as a rare treat. The trees in the orchards were bare, but apple juice stored away in oak barrels had fermented to a delightfully sparkling cider. And the spices we take for granted — cinnamon bark, whole nutmeg and cardamom pods — were rare delicacies. ※ Now, with fresh fruit flown in from warmer climates as much a part of our holiday menu as dried fruit, we may ask, why bother making fruitcakes at all? I make them *because* they take time and patience. They give me a change of pace from my hectic life and they remind me that good things are worth waiting for.

STEAMED PUDDINGS AND SAUCES

· ·

Christmas is the only time we tend to make these very traditional, Dickensian desserts despite the fact that they are really simple to prepare and require no special equipment.

When I steam my plum puddings (recipe following), I use every large pot in the kitchen and a variety of small containers from bowls and mugs to tin cans. Anything can be used as a mold as long as the top opening is as wide as the sides, so the pudding will slide out easily after steaming.

Butter the inside of the molds and fill them three-quarters full with pudding batter. Cover them with a double layer of waxed paper held closed with a layer of aluminum foil or tied with a piece of string.

To steam puddings, use one or more Dutch ovens or large pots with close-fitting lids. Perforated steamers are the best way to prop up the pudding molds above the level of the boiling water. But, if necessary, improvise with cooling racks, colanders, plates or forks. Make sure the steam circulates as freely as possible around the molds. Keep two or three inches of simmering water in the pot at all times. Add more boiling water as needed.

After steaming, remove the puddings from the large pots, remove the waxed paper or metal mold covers and allow the molds to cool for ten minutes. Invert the molds, remove the puddings and allow them to cool completely. Wrap them well in plastic (aluminum foil may corrode from the moisture). Refrigerate plum puddings up to two months. After that, store them in the freezer. Other puddings can be refrigerated two weeks before freezing.

To reheat, butter original mold and place pudding in it. Cover with aluminum foil and resteam for about one hour. Small pieces can be covered with plastic wrap and cooked for one or two minutes in a microwave oven.

· ·

MY FAVORITE PLUM PUDDING

The first plum pudding I ever tasted was this wonderful Newfoundland recipe from Robyn Randall Zuck. I make it faithfully every Christmas.

¾ lb	candied cherries	375 g
13 oz	raisins	375 g
1 lb	currants	500 g
½ lb	candied mixed peel	250 g
¼ lb	chopped dates	125 g
2½ cups	white flour	625 mL
1½ cups	minced suet	375 mL
4	eggs	4
2 cups	molasses	500 mL
2 cups	cultured buttermilk	500 mL
1 cup	rum	250 mL
½ cup	freshly squeezed lemon juice	125 mL
2 tsp	vanilla	10 mL
½ cup	milk	125 mL
2½ cups	fine dry bread crumbs	625 mL
1 tsp	cloves	5 mL
1 tsp	allspice	5 mL
1 tsp	nutmeg	5 mL
1 tsp	cinnamon	5 mL
1 tsp	salt	5 mL
2 tsp	baking soda	10 mL

In a very large bowl, mix together cherries, raisins, currants, peel, dates, ½ cup (125 mL) flour and suet. In another large bowl, beat eggs until light. Stir in molasses, buttermilk, rum, lemon juice, vanilla and milk. Stir in bread crumbs. Stir liquid mixture into fruit mixture until blended. Sift together remaining flour, spices, salt and baking soda into medium bowl. Stir flour mixture into fruit mixture. Pour into 4 buttered 1-qt (1 L) molds and steam 3 or more hours, until top is firm to the touch. Cool and store. Serve with hard sauce (see recipes, pages 8 and 9). **YIELD: 4 qt (4 L)**

CARROT PUDDING

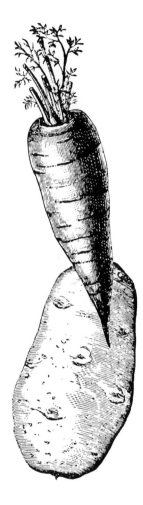

Molly Titus's family loves this recipe because it is not as sweet as plum pudding. As it does not have the keeping quality of plum pudding, let it mellow a week or two in the refrigerator and then freeze it until Christmas. Defrost before resteaming.

1 cup	white flour	250 mL
¼ tsp	salt	1 mL
¼ tsp	cloves	1 mL
¼ tsp	cinnamon	1 mL
¾ tsp	nutmeg	3 mL
1 tsp	baking soda	5 mL
1 cup	raisins	250 mL
1 cup	currants	250 mL
¼ cup	whole candied cherries	50 mL
¼ cup	finely chopped candied citron	50 mL
¼ cup	slivered almonds	50 mL
½ cup	butter	125 mL
½ cup	brown sugar	125 mL
1	egg	1
1 cup	grated carrot	250 mL
1 cup	grated potato	250 mL

Sift flour, salt, cloves, cinnamon, nutmeg and baking soda into large bowl. Stir in raisins, currants, cherries, citron and almonds. In another large bowl, cream butter and brown sugar together. Beat in egg, carrot and potato. Combine butter and flour mixtures and press into large buttered mold. Cover and steam 2 hours. Serve with hard sauce (see recipes, pages 8 and 9). **YIELD: 8 cups (2 L)**

KATHY'S INDIVIDUAL CRANBERRY PUDDINGS

. . . .

My friend Kathy Chute picks bushels of cranberries from the bogs around us and then makes this scrumptious dessert saturated with Cranberry Pudding Sauce (recipe follows).

½ cup	molasses	125 mL
½ cup	boiling water	125 mL
2 tsp	baking soda	10 mL
1⅓ cups	white flour	325 mL
1 tsp	baking powder	5 mL
¼ tsp	salt	1 mL
2 cups	coarsely chopped fresh cranberries	500 mL
½ cup	coarsely chopped pecans	125 mL

In medium bowl, combine molasses and boiling water. Stir in baking soda. Sift together flour, baking powder and salt. Stir flour mixture, cranberries and pecans into molasses mixture until well combined. Pour into 8 buttered 1-cup (250 mL) molds such as Pyrex custard cups. Cover with aluminum foil. Steam 30 to 45 minutes until puffed up and cooked through. Serve with Cranberry Pudding Sauce.   **YIELD: 8 servings**

. . . .

CRANBERRY PUDDING SAUCE

. . . .

½ cup	butter	125 mL
1 cup	white sugar	250 mL
1 cup	heavy cream	250 mL
1 tsp	vanilla	5 mL

Melt butter in heavy-bottomed small saucepan, over low heat. Stir in sugar and cream and simmer 10 minutes.

To microwave: combine all ingredients in small microwave safe bowl. Cook on Medium 2 to 5 minutes until slightly thickened. Serve hot over puddings.   **YIELD: 1 cup (250 mL)**

. . . .

HARD SAUCES

· ·

Hard sauces are hard only while they are cold. Put them on a steaming hot pudding and they melt into a butter-rich sauce. After combining all the ingredients, place the sauce in a small bowl and refrigerate it up to a week before serving. My friend Phyllis Emerson, who grew up in New England, remembers being enchanted as a child by the rose-tinted sauce stars on her cranberry pudding. Her mother made them by spreading hard sauce on a cookie sheet, chilling it until it hardened, and then cutting it out with a star-shaped cookie cutter.

· ·

Brown Sugar Hard Sauce

1	egg	1
3 tbsp	melted butter	50 mL
1 cup	brown sugar	250 mL
½ tsp	vanilla	2 mL
1 cup	heavy cream	250 mL

In small bowl, beat together egg, butter, brown sugar and vanilla. In large bowl, whip cream until stiff. Gently fold egg mixture into whipped cream.   **YIELD: 3 cups (750 mL)**

· ·

Vanilla Hard Sauce

¼ cup	butter	50 mL
1 cup	icing sugar	250 mL
1 tsp	vanilla	5 mL
1-2 tbsp	heavy cream	15-25 mL

In small bowl, cream butter by hand or with electric mixer until light and fluffy. Beat in icing sugar and vanilla and enough cream to make a soft sauce.   **YIELD: 1 cup (250 mL)**

· ·

Brandy Hard Sauce

¼ cup	butter	50 mL
1 cup	icing sugar	250 mL
2-3 tbsp	brandy	25-50 mL

In small bowl, cream butter by hand or with electric mixer until light and fluffy. Beat in icing sugar and enough brandy to make a soft sauce.   **YIELD: 1 cup (250 mL)**

. . . .

Orange Hard Sauce

¼ cup	butter	50 mL
1 cup	icing sugar	250 mL
1 tsp	grated orange rind	5 mL
1-2 tbsp	freshly squeezed orange juice OR orange liqueur	(15-25 mL)

In small bowl, cream butter by hand or with electric mixer until light and fluffy. Beat in icing sugar, orange rind and enough juice or liqueur to make a soft sauce.   **YIELD: 1 cup (250 mL)**

. . . .

COOKIES THAT KEEP

Most cookies are best eaten within a few days of baking, but some actually improve with age. Many traditional European Christmas cookies are heavy with honey and spices and remind us of the gifts the Magi brought to the Christ Child. Although our modern palates are accustomed to sweeter cookies, these take us back to a time when *sugar and spice* were a rare treat.

LEBKUCHEN — GERMAN HONEY SPICE COOKIES

Lebkuchen are traditionally rolled out and cut into bars. In this easier version the dough is baked in one piece on a sided cookie sheet and then cut while still warm from the oven.

2	eggs	2
¾ cup	honey	175 mL
¼ cup	molasses	50 mL
½ cup	milk	125 mL
2½ cups	white flour	625 mL
½ cup	white sugar	125 mL
½ tsp	baking powder	2 mL
½ tsp	cinnamon	2 mL
¼ tsp	nutmeg	1 mL
½ tsp	cloves OR allspice	2 mL
½ cup	minced combination of candied orange peel, lemon peel and citron	125 mL
1 cup	finely ground almonds OR hazelnuts	250 mL

Glaze

1 cup	icing sugar	250 mL
½ tsp	vanilla, almond extract OR rum	2 mL
1-2 tsp	freshly squeezed lemon juice	5-10 mL
1 tbsp	water	15 mL

Preheat oven to 400°F (200°C). Beat eggs, honey, molasses and milk in large bowl. Sift flour, sugar, baking powder and spices into another large bowl. Stir in candied fruit and nuts. With wooden spoon, beat egg mixture into flour mixture. Using a knife, spread dough evenly into buttered and floured, 14 × 10 in (35 × 25 cm) jelly-roll pan or cookie sheet with sides. Bake 12 to 15 minutes, until edges are brown and cookies are firm to touch.

To prepare glaze, sift icing sugar into small bowl and stir in remaining ingredients until smooth. Set aside.

Remove cookie sheet from oven. Place a wire cooling rack upside down on top of the cookies and invert. Cool 2 minutes and turn out onto a wooden cutting board. Brush on glaze while still warm and cut into 1 × 2 in (2.5 × 5 cm) bars. Remove to cooling rack and cool thoroughly. Wrap and store in cookie tin. Allow to mellow at least 2 to 3 days before serving.

YIELD: about 6 dozen

A glaze is a paste of icing sugar (8 parts) and water (1 part) thick enough to coat the back of a spoon. Substituting liquid flavorings (such as lemon juice, vanilla, almond extract or rum) for the water makes it more tasty. The glaze is brushed on the warm cookies and hardens when they cool.

SIX-WEEK BUTTER-NUT COOKIES

My friend, who generously contributed this recipe, has made these cookies six weeks before Christmas every year, for over 35 years. When she was just a bride, she got the recipe from a Greek neighbor.

2 cups	soft butter	500 mL
⅔ cup	white sugar	150 mL
2 cups	finely chopped pecans OR walnuts	500 mL
1 tbsp	vanilla	15 mL
4 cups	sifted white flour	1 L
2 cups	icing sugar (optional)	500 mL

When cookie recipes specify a varying amount of flour, add the minimum amount first; then bake a test cookie. If the cookie spreads more than it should, add a few tablespoons of flour. If too much flour is added, however, the cookie may crack. The best way to soften the dough is with a little cream.

Preheat oven to 375°F (190°C). Cream butter and sugar in large bowl with electric mixer until light and fluffy. Beat in nuts and vanilla by hand. Sift, then measure flour and beat into butter mixture. Wrap and chill dough in refrigerator until stiff enough to shape with hands. Place dough, 1 tsp (5 mL) at a time, in hand; shape into balls and flatten to make 1 to 1½ in (2.5 to 3.75 cm) cookies. Place on ungreased cookie sheets and bake 8 to 10 minutes until light brown. Sift icing sugar onto a platter and dredge both sides of warm cookies in it. Store cookies in a foil-lined wooden box or cookie tin with sheets of foil between layers. Sprinkle on additional icing sugar if desired at serving. **YIELD: about 7 dozen**

SHORTBREAD

Traditional shortbread is a rich biscuit served in wedges on Hogmanay or New Year's Eve in Scotland. There are many variations, but true shortbread is a thick cookie made of two parts white flour, one part butter and a small amount of white sugar. While some cooks may vary the flour (white, whole wheat, semolina, rice), and the sugar (white, brown, icing, or superfine), most people agree that the shortening must be butter.

Other additions which have become popular over the years include: cornstarch, eggs, milk, vanilla extract, almond extract and grated lemon peel.

Traditional shortbread is made by sifting together the flour and sugar and then rubbing and kneading in the butter by hand. It is less messy to cream the butter and sugar and then knead in the flour. The texture of shortbread will vary depending on the type and amount of flour and added moisture. Some people roll out and cut the dough into individual cookies. Others pat it into one large flat cookie circle and bake it on a cookie sheet or in the bottom of a round cake pan or pie plate. This method is best when the dough is crumbly. Sticky dough can be rolled between layers of waxed paper. Cookie thickness varies from ¼ to 1 in (6 mm to 2.5 cm).

Before baking the larger cookies, prick them with a fork to allow steam to escape so the shape won't warp. Decorate shortbread with everything from candied fruit and peel or nuts to jam and chocolate sprinkles.

What it comes down to is that people like the shortbread they know best, usually the kind that their mothers made. Here is a collection of some mothers' best shortbread recipes.

WENDY'S MOTHER'S FINE SUGAR SHORTBREAD

. . . .

1 cup	butter	250 mL
½ cup	superfine sugar	125 mL
2 cups	sifted white flour	500 mL

Preheat oven to 275°F (140°C). Using an electric mixer, beat butter in large bowl until fluffy. Beat in sugar gradually; add flour and shape into a ball. Place dough between 2 layers of waxed paper and roll out to ⅓ in (8 mm) thick. Cut out with cookie cutters. Place on ungreased cookie sheets and bake 25 to 30 minutes. Do not allow to brown.   **YIELD: 2½ dozen**

Store soft cookies in tins or jars, with a slice of apple added to keep them moist. Crisp cookies should be kept in boxes — or freeze them so they'll stay fresh.

. . . .

SEMOLINA SHORTBREAD

. . . .

Semolina flour, made from hard durum wheat, produces a slightly gritty, dense shortbread much like the imported commercial kind. It is excellent for shaping into a large round.

½ cup	butter	125 mL
¼ cup	white sugar	50 mL
1 cup	white flour	250 mL
¼ cup	semolina flour	50 mL

Preheat oven to 325°F (160°C). In a large bowl, cream butter and sugar. Add flours and knead to form a ball. Pat into bottom of a 9-in (22.5-cm) pie plate or cake pan or roll into a 9-in (22.5-cm) circle on cookie sheet. Pierce with a fork and lightly score into 12 even wedges. Bake 25 to 35 minutes. Allow to cool slightly and harden before removing to cooling rack.
YIELD: 12 wedges

. . . .

RICE FLOUR SHORTBREAD

1 cup	butter	250 mL
½ cup	white sugar	125 mL
1 tsp	vanilla	5 mL
1½ cups	white flour	375 mL
⅔ cup	rice flour	150 mL

Preheat oven to 325°F (160°C). In a large bowl, cream butter and sugar and beat in vanilla. Sift flours together and mix flour into butter mixture to form 2 balls. Knead dough until well mixed and pat into the bottom of two 9-in (22.5 cm) pie plates. Pierce with fork and gently score each cookie into 12 even wedges, or roll between 2 layers of waxed paper and cut into individual cookies. Bake 25 to 30 minutes until golden brown. Invert onto rack to cool. **YIELD: 12 wedges or 4 dozen small cookies**

MY MOTHER'S SHORTBREAD

This brown sugar cookie has a rich color and taste. The dough is very pliant and can be cut into individual cookies or shaped into huge alphabet cookies.

1 cup	butter	250 mL
½ cup	brown sugar	125 mL
1 tsp	vanilla	5 mL
2 cups	white flour	500 mL

Preheat oven to 375°F (190°C). Cream butter in a large bowl; blend in brown sugar, vanilla and white flour. Form into a ball and roll out on a lightly floured surface to ¼ in (6 mm) thick. Cut dough into squares or use cookie cutter shapes and decorate if desired. Place on ungreased cookie sheet and bake 10 to 15 minutes, until golden brown.   **YIELD: 2½ dozen**

Food Processor Method
Cream butter in food processor with metal blade. Add brown sugar, vanilla and flour. Process until ball is formed. Put dough on large ungreased cookie sheet. Pat into a ball and roll into a 10 in (25 cm) circle. Score wedges in dough, leaving pieces in place and pierce with fork. Bake 10 to 15 minutes, until golden brown. Cool on cookie sheet and break off wedges to serve.

SHORTBREAD LETTERS

For fun, my children and I mix up a large double batch of shortbread. They love mixing it with their hands and usually have dough up to their elbows. We roll the dough into half a dozen 7 in (17.5 cm) circles, about ⅜-in (8 cm) thick. Removing as little dough as possible, we form letters and bake them 12 to 15 minutes until light brown. After they cool, we wrap them in aluminum foil and the children give the huge alphabet cookies to their friends as Christmas presents.   **YIELD: 4 dozen**

SIX-WEEK BUTTER-NUT COOKIES *(see page 12)*
with LAST-MINUTE FRUIT CAKE *(see page 119)*

FRUITCAKES

People either love or hate fruitcake. Both groups, however, feel obligated to politely nibble at it every year. But fruitcake is just too much work to make if you feel ambiguous on the subject. If you prefer chocolate cake with chocolate icing, why not make it a Christmas tradition in your house?

If you decide to take the time to make fruitcake this year, here are some helpful hints: Divide the work into a two-day process. Chop all the fruit and nuts and dredge them in a little flour the first day. The second day, combine the ingredients and bake the cakes. It does not seem like as much trouble this way, especially when you have a friend over to sip coffee and chat while you work.

For years I was intimidated by complicated instructions for lining pans with parchment and wrapping cakes in brandy-soaked linen. Now, I simply line loaf pans with generous lengths of buttered waxed paper, pour in the batter, fold the excess paper in a butcher's fold over the top of the batter, and bake them. The waxed paper protects the top from browning. When the cakes are done, I pull them out of the pans and peel off the paper. When the cakes are cool, I sprinkle on two or three tablespoons of brandy and wrap them in plastic wrap.

FINNISH FIG CAKE

· ·

Baked in a large bundt pan, this cake takes on a Christmas wreath shape. It keeps well in the refrigerator for a week or two.

½ cup	orange juice	125 mL
½ cup	chopped soft Calimyrna figs	125 mL
2 tbsp	ground almonds	25 mL
1½ cups	white flour	375 mL
1 tsp	baking powder	5 mL
½ cup	raisins	125 mL
¼ cup	chopped walnuts	50 mL
2 tbsp	grated orange peel	25 mL
¾ cup	butter	175 mL
¾ cup	brown sugar	175 mL
2	eggs	2
2 tbsp	icing sugar	25 mL

Preheat oven to 350°F (180°C). Place orange juice in a small saucepan over medium heat and bring almost to a boil. Remove from heat, add figs and set aside to cool. Butter a ring mold, tube or bundt pan. Sprinkle almonds evenly on bottom and sides of pan. In a medium bowl, sift together flour and baking powder and stir in raisins, walnuts and 1 tbsp (15 mL) grated orange peel. In a large bowl, cream butter and brown sugar and beat in eggs, 1 at a time. Blend flour and fig mixtures alternately into butter mixture. Spoon into prepared pan and bake 35 to 40 minutes or until a toothpick comes out dry and crumb-free. Do not overbake. Remove from pan. Allow to cool 10 minutes before inverting on a cooling rack. Wrap and age overnight. To serve, dust with icing sugar and remaining orange peel.   **YIELD: 1 small cake**

· ·

DARK DRIED FRUITCAKE

. . . .

I have mixed feelings about the rubbery, fluorescent-colored glacéed fruits used in many fruitcakes. That's why I prefer these recipes which use dried fruit mix, instead. Choose any combination of dried banana chips, coconut, apricots, apples, papaya, pineapple, etc. The cakes are moist and not overly sweet.

Fruitcake cannot be rushed by increasing the heat. Above 300°F (150°C), the cakes tend to brown and dry out and raisins take on a burned flavor. To retard the drying process, some bakers place a pan of hot water in the oven underneath the cakes.

½ cup	molasses	125 mL
¼ cup	water	50 mL
1 cup	raisins	250 mL
1 cup	chopped dates	250 mL
2 cups	coarsely chopped dried fruit mix	500 mL
1 cup	white flour	250 mL
1 tsp	cinnamon	5 mL
½ tsp	nutmeg	2 mL
½ tsp	ginger	2 mL
¼ tsp	baking soda	1 mL
1½ cups	pecan AND/OR walnut pieces	375 mL
½ cup	butter	125 mL
½ cup	white sugar	125 mL
3	eggs	3
1 tsp	freshly grated orange rind	5 mL
¼ cup	orange juice	50 mL
½ cup	brandy (apple brandy is best) for moistening cake	125 mL
¼ cup	apricot jam	50 mL
6	dried apricots for decoration	6

Preheat oven to 275°F (140°C). In medium saucepan, stir together molasses and water and bring to a boil over medium heat. Stir in raisins and dates, reduce heat and simmer uncovered 5 minutes. Remove from heat; stir in dried fruit mix and set aside to cool. Sift flour, spices and baking soda into medium bowl and stir in nuts. In a large bowl, cream butter and sugar. Beat in eggs, orange rind and orange juice. Blend flour and butter mixtures. Fold in molasses mixture. Pour into a large 9 × 5 in (22.5 × 12.5 cm) loaf pan lined with buttered waxed paper. Fold paper over top. Bake about 2 hours until firm to the touch. Immediately remove cake from loaf pan and cool on rack. After 5 minutes peel off waxed paper and allow to cool completely. Drizzle 2 tbsp (25 mL) brandy on all sides of cake and wrap in plastic. Allow to age in cool spot for at least 2 weeks. Drizzle on 2 or 3 tbsp (25 or 50 mL) of brandy every week or so until served. To serve, glaze cake with warmed apricot jam and garnish with dried apricots.   **YIELD: 1 cake**

To flame a fruitcake or dessert, dip several cubes of sugar in a small amount of lemon extract, then place on dessert. Light it immediately and you should have a lovely blue flame!

· ·

NUTTY FRUITCAKE

· ·

This cake is rich with nuts but not shortening. The fruit provides a juicy contrast to the nuts.

½ cup	white flour	125 mL
½ cup	white sugar	125 mL
1 tsp	baking powder	5 mL
½ tsp	nutmeg OR cinnamon	2 mL
3 cups	chopped pecans AND/OR walnuts	750 mL
¾ cup	halved candied cherries	175 mL
1 cup	chopped candied pineapple	250 mL
2	eggs	2
1 tsp	vanilla	5 mL

Preheat oven to 250°F (120°C). In a large bowl, sift together flour, sugar, baking powder and nutmeg or cinnamon. Stir in nuts and fruit. In a small bowl, whisk together eggs and vanilla and stir into flour mixture. Press into small 3.5 × 7.5 in (8.75 × 18.75 cm) loaf pan lined with buttered waxed paper. Fold over top and bake 1 to 1½ hours, until firm to the touch. Remove cake from loaf pan and cool on rack immediately. After 5 minutes peel off waxed paper and allow to cool completely. Wrap well in plastic.   **YIELD: 1 cake**

· ·

GOLDEN DRIED FRUITCAKE

½ cup	corn syrup	125 mL
¼ cup	water	50 mL
4 cups	coarsely chopped dried fruit mix (see recipe introduction, page 20)	1 L
1 cup	white flour	250 mL
1 tsp	cinnamon	5 mL
½ tsp	nutmeg	2 mL
½ tsp	cloves	2 mL
¼ tsp	baking soda	1 mL
1½ cups	pecan AND/OR walnut pieces	375 mL
½ cup	butter	125 mL
½ cup	white sugar	125 mL
3	eggs	3
1 tsp	freshly grated orange rind	5 mL
¼ cup	orange juice	50 mL
½ cup	brandy (apple is best)	125 mL
¼ cup	apple jelly	50 mL
3-4	dried apple rings for decoration	3-4

Preheat oven to 275°F (140°C). In medium saucepan, stir together corn syrup and water and bring to a boil over medium heat. Remove from heat and stir in dried fruit mix. Set aside to cool. In a medium bowl, sift together flour, spices and baking soda and stir in nuts. In a large bowl, cream butter and sugar. Beat in eggs, orange rind and orange juice. Blend flour and butter mixtures. Fold in fruit mixture and pour into a large 9 × 5 in (22.5 × 12.5 cm) loaf pan lined with buttered waxed paper. Fold paper over top. Bake about 2 hours until firm to the touch. Immediately remove cake from loaf pan and cool on rack. After 5 minutes peel off waxed paper and allow to cool completely. Drizzle 2 tbsp (25 mL) brandy on all sides of cake and wrap in plastic. Allow to age in cool spot for at least 2 weeks. Drizzle on 2 or 3 tbsp (25 or 50 mL) of brandy every week or so until served. To serve, glaze cake with warmed apple jelly and garnish with dried apple rings.   **YIELD: 1 cake**

UKRAINIAN CHRISTMAS
HONEY CAKE

· ·

1 cup	white sugar	250 mL
1 cup	vegetable oil	250 mL
3	eggs	3
1 cup	honey, preferably buckwheat	250 mL
3 cups	white flour	750 mL
2 tsp	baking powder	10 mL
1 tsp	baking soda	5 mL
½ tsp	cinnamon	2 mL
½ tsp	cloves OR allspice	2 mL
1 cup	raisins	250 mL
1 cup	chopped dates OR figs	250 mL
1 cup	chopped walnuts	250 mL
1 cup	cold strong coffee	250 mL
½ cup	honey	125 mL
6	walnut halves	6
6	glacéed cherries	6

Foods containing honey have a tendency to brown rapidly when baking, so watch them closely to prevent burning.

Preheat oven to 300°F (150°C). In large bowl, beat together sugar, oil, eggs and honey. In another large bowl, sift together flour, baking powder, baking soda and spices. Stir in raisins, dates or figs and walnuts. Add flour mixture to honey mixture alternately with coffee. Pour into a buttered and floured 9 × 14 in (22.5 × 35 cm) pan. Bake 1 to 1½ hours until a toothpick inserted in the middle comes out dry and crumb-free. Remove from oven and glaze cake with warmed honey. Decorate with walnut halves and cherries dipped in honey. Remove from pan, wrap well and store at least 1 week in refrigerator.   **YIELD: 1 cake**

· ·

CAKES FOR THE FREEZER

. . . .

CHERRY POUND CAKE

. . . .

This is the best pound cake I have ever eaten. Claire Bird of Liverpool, Nova Scotia, bakes dozens of cakes in November and freezes them for Christmas presents.

1½ cups	maraschino cherries, drained	375 mL
½ cup	slivered almonds	125 mL
½ cup	minced candied citron	125 mL
4 cups	white flour	1 L
2 tsp	baking powder	5 mL
1½ cups	butter at room temperature	375 mL
2 cups	white sugar	500 mL
4	eggs	4
1 cup	milk	250 mL
2 tsp	vanilla	10 mL
1 tsp	almond extract	5 mL
1 tsp	lemon extract	5 mL

Preheat oven to 325°F (160°C). In medium bowl, place maraschino cherries, almonds and citron and stir in ¼ cup (50 mL) flour. In a separate bowl, sift together remaining flour and baking powder. In large bowl, cream butter and sugar and beat in eggs. Continue beating, with electric mixer, until very light and fluffy, at least 5 to 6 minutes. Combine milk, vanilla, almond and lemon extracts in small bowl. Beat flour mixture into butter mixture alternately with milk mixture. Fold maraschino cherry mixture into batter and pour into buttered large tube or bundt pan. Bake 1½ to 2 hours until a toothpick comes out dry and crumb-free. Invert on a cooling rack. Cool, wrap well in plastic and freeze.   **YIELD: 1 large cake**

. . . .

DATE NUT CHOCOLATE CHUNK LOAF

This is my husband's favorite Christmas bread.

1 cup	chopped dates	250 mL
1 cup	boiling water	250 mL
1 tsp	baking soda	5 mL
½ cup	butter	125 mL
½ cup	vegetable shortening	125 mL
¾ cup	white sugar	175 mL
2	eggs	2
1 tsp	vanilla	5 mL
2 cups	white flour	500 mL
3 tbsp	cocoa	50 mL
3 oz (3 squares)	semi-sweet chocolate	85 g
½ cup	coarsely chopped walnuts	125 mL

Preheat oven to 350°F (180°C). Place dates in a small bowl; add boiling water and baking soda, to soften. Set aside to cool. In a large bowl, cream butter, vegetable shortening and sugar. Beat in eggs and vanilla. In small bowl, sift together flour and cocoa. Combine flour, butter and date mixtures. Coarsely chop chocolate and add to batter along with walnuts. Pour into two, 3½ × 7½ in (8.75 × 18.75 cm) buttered loaf pans. Bake 45 minutes, until a toothpick comes out dry and crumb-free.
YIELD: 2 small loaves

MINCEMEAT

. . . .

Christmas would not be Christmas in Britain without mince pies. Although the British stopped putting meat in their mincemeat years ago, North Americans, especially rural ones with access to wild meat, still do. My neighbor Eric Holden recalls that as a boy the tradition in his family was to eat one mince tart a day during the 12 days of Christmas. It was thought to bring good luck in each month of the new year. His wife Mary remembers eating 12 different kinds of fruitcake for the same reason.

. . . .

MEATLESS MINCEMEAT
. . . .

2 cups	raisins	500 mL
1 cup	currants	250 mL
½ cup	coarsely chopped dried apricots	125 mL
1 cup	minced suet	250 mL
3	peeled chopped apples	3
½ cup	marmalade	125 mL
¾ cup	slivered almonds AND/OR pecans	175 mL
1 cup	brown sugar	250 mL
½ cup	candied peel	125 mL
½	lemon — juice and grated rind	½
½ tsp	freshly grated lemon peel	2 mL
½ cup	brandy OR sherry OR bourbon	125 mL
¼ tsp	cinnamon	1 mL
¼ tsp	freshly grated whole nutmeg	1 mL
¼ tsp	allspice	1 mL
¼ tsp	mace	1 mL

In large bowl, mix together all ingredients. Place in a large jar or crock. Cover and refrigerate at least 3 weeks before using. Stir once a week and add more brandy, sherry or bourbon as it is absorbed. Will keep up to 2 months or more.
YIELD: 2 qt (2 L), enough for 3 pies

. . . .

HEARTY COOKED MINCEMEAT

1 lb	finely ground lean beef OR venison*	500 g
4 cups	apple juice OR grape juice	1 L
1 tsp	cinnamon	5 mL
1 tsp	mace	5 mL
1 tsp	cloves OR allspice	5 mL
1 tsp	grated whole nutmeg	5 mL
¼ cup	butter	50 mL
1½ cups	white sugar	375 mL
1 cup	finely minced suet	250 mL
4	apples, peeled, cored and coarsely chopped	4
2½ cups	raisins	625 mL
2 cups	currants	500 mL
1½ cups	mixed candied peel (orange, lemon, citron)	375 mL
1	lemon — juice and rind	1
1	orange — juice and rind	1
2 cups	pecans OR walnuts OR almonds	500 mL
2 cups	fresh whole cranberries	500 mL
½ or more cup	brandy OR sherry OR bourbon	125 mL

*Heart or round steak are best.

Place meat, juice and spices in large kettle or Dutch oven. Bring to a boil. Stir in remaining ingredients except liquor. Continue cooking uncovered over medium-low heat, stirring occasionally for 1 hour. Remove from heat. Stir in liquor and pour into sterile canning jars, leaving 1 in (2.5 cm) headspace. Seal and process in a pressure canner at 10 lb (4.5 kg) pressure for 20 minutes.   **YIELD: 3 to 4 qt (3 to 4 L), enough for 5 pies**

Because of the meat content, we recommend sealing and heat processing this mincemeat in canning jars. You can store it in the refrigerator for a few weeks without processing, but add more brandy, sherry or bourbon to prevent bacterial growth.

THE SPIRIT OF HOMEMADE LIQUEURS

. . . .

Getting into the Christmas spirit with homemade liqueurs is as simple as putting alcohol and flavoring into a bottle and letting it sit a month or two. The liquid is then strained and mixed with Sugar Syrup (recipe follows). I use flavorless alcool or vodka, but any spirit of 40 per cent alcohol or more will do. Whiskey, brandy, gin, rum or eau de vie add their own flavor and prevent spoilage from bacteria. A 1 L bottle of alcohol is enough to make 1 cup (250 mL) each of four different kinds of liqueur.

. . . .

SUGAR SYRUP

. . . .

This is a basic ingredient of all homemade liqueurs. You don't need to prepare it until the alcohol has been strained.

2 cups	white sugar	500 mL
1 cup	water	250 mL

Combine all ingredients in medium saucepan over medium-high heat and bring to a boil for 5 minutes. Set aside to cool and bottle until ready to use.   **YIELD: 1 cup (250 mL)**

. . . .

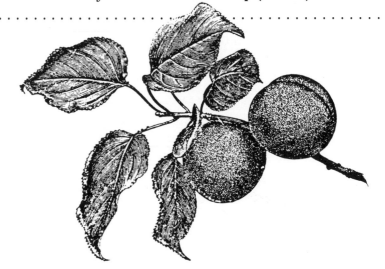

CRANBERRY

· ·

An intensely red, fragrant, fruity liqueur.

2 cups	fresh whole cranberries	500 mL
1 tsp	grated orange rind	5 mL
1 cup	vodka OR alcool	250 mL
⅓ cup	Sugar Syrup (page 28)	75 mL

Coarsely chop cranberries and place in large jar. Add orange rind and vodka or alcool. Seal tightly with a double layer of waxed paper and a lid. Shake well and store in a cool spot for a month, shaking contents from time to time. Strain liquid; save solids and pour liquid into a clean bottle. Stir in sugar syrup. Cover and store indefinitely at room temperature. Add some sugar to sweeten the leftover cranberries and use as a very different kind of cranberry sauce.   **YIELD: 1½ cups (375 mL)**

· ·

DRIED APRICOT

· ·

A thick, smooth, apricot-colored liqueur.

1 cup	boiling water	250 mL
1 cup	dried apricots	250 mL
3	almonds	3
1 cup	vodka OR alcool	250 mL
3-4 tbsp	Sugar Syrup (page 28)	50-60 mL

Pour boiling water over apricots in small bowl. Set aside for 5 minutes. Drain and place in large jar. Add almonds and vodka or alcool. Seal tightly with a double layer of waxed paper and a lid. Shake well and store in a cool spot for a month, shaking contents from time to time. Strain liquid; save apricots and pour liquid into a clean bottle. Stir in sugar syrup. Cover and store indefinitely at room temperature. Add sugar or sugar syrup to apricots for an easy dessert, with ice cream, in a fruit bread, or as the basis of fruit compote.   **YIELD: ¾ cup (175 mL)**

· ·

COFFEE

. . . .

A maple brown, slightly bitter liqueur.

¼ cup	coffee beans	50 mL
1 tsp	vanilla	5 mL
	OR	
1	vanilla bean	1
1 cup	vodka OR alcool	250 mL
¾ cup	Sugar Syrup (page 28)	175 mL

Combine coffee beans, vanilla and vodka or alcool in large jar. Seal tightly with a double layer of waxed paper and a lid. Shake well and store in a cool spot for 2 days only. Strain liquid; discard solids and pour liquid into a clean bottle. Stir in sugar syrup. Cover and store indefinitely at room temperature. **YIELD: 1⅓ cups (325 mL)**

. . . .

ANISE/LICORICE

. . . .

A dark yellow, aromatic liqueur.

2 tsp	star anise	10 mL
1 cup	vodka OR alcool	250 mL
½ cup	Sugar Syrup (page 28)	125 mL

Combine star anise and vodka or alcool in large jar. Seal tightly with a double layer of waxed paper and a lid. Shake well and store in a cool spot for 2 days only. Strain liquid; discard solids and pour liquid into a clean bottle. Stir in sugar syrup. Cover and store indefinitely at room temperature. **YIELD: 1⅓ cups (325 mL)**

. . . .

APPLE

· ·

A golden orange, perfumey liqueur.

2 cups	finely chopped unpeeled apples	500 mL
1 in	cinnamon stick	2.5 cm
2	whole allspice	2
1 cup	vodka OR alcool	250 mL
¼ cup	Sugar Syrup (page 28)	50 mL

Combine apples, cinnamon stick, allspice and vodka or alcool in large jar. Seal tightly with a double layer of waxed paper and a lid. Shake well and store in a cool spot for a month. Shake contents from time to time. Strain liquid; discard solids and pour liquid into a clean bottle. Stir in sugar syrup. Cover and store indefinitely at room temperature.
YIELD: 1 cup (250 mL)

· ·

BOERENJONGENS
· ·

This Dutch raisin liqueur translates as "farmer's boys", and we can only hazard a guess as to how it got its name. You can substitute dried apricots for the raisins to make Boerenmeisjes, "farmer's girls."

1 cup	raisins	250 mL
1 in	cinnamon stick	2.5 cm
¼ cup	white sugar	50 mL
¼ cup	boiling water	50 mL
¾ cup	brandy	175 mL

Place raisins, cinnamon stick and sugar in clean glass jar. Add boiling water; cover and set aside 24 hours. Add brandy, stir, cover and set aside for at least 2 weeks. Serve raisins and brandy together in small glasses with a spoon or as a topping for ice cream.   **YIELD: 2 cups (500 mL)**

· ·

WINTER FRUIT COMPOTE

This refreshing light dessert should be prepared a few days before serving and kept in the refrigerator. Small bottles make nice Christmas presents.

2 cups	prunes	500 mL
2 cups	dried apricots	500 mL
½ cup	raisins	125 mL
6-7 cups	apple juice, divided	1.5-1.75 L
2 in	cinnamon stick	5 cm
2	oranges	2
2	apples	2
1	lemon	1
1	grapefruit	1
½-¾ cup	light rum OR brandy	125-175 mL

In very large bowl, place prunes, apricots and raisins. In large saucepan, bring 4 cups (1 L) apple juice and cinnamon stick to a boil over high heat. Pour over fruit. Set aside to cool. Prepare fresh fruit by cutting into interesting shapes. Peel, section and remove membranes from one orange and the grapefruit. Slice other orange, including peel, into very thin rounds (discarding seeds). Cut lemon into tiny wedges. Cut apples, peel intact, with melon baller, or slice into wedges with knife. Add chopped fresh fruit and rum or brandy to bowl. Blend and pour into small bottles. Top with apple juice. Seal and refrigerate overnight. The flavor improves with age. It will keep 4 or 5 days. Serve as is, or on top of ice cream.   **YIELD: 3 qt (3 L)**

POTTED CHEESE *(see page 44)*
with SPICY NUTS *(see page 48)*

*I*nvited guests are fun, but for me, Christmas is all about unexpected company: the old high school boyfriend who calls and wants to stop by in 15 minutes and the I'll-be-home-for-Christmas relatives. ◼ Since the stores are brimming with unusual inventory like kumquats and pecans in the North and cranberries and balsam fir wreaths in the South, it is a great time to stock the larder for impromptu guests. It is a delicious feeling to splurge on a few extras, to indulge ourselves a little. ◼ With stocked shelves and a few extras in the refrigerator and freezer, I can quickly whip together some savory tidbits for my friends. Cultures all over the world have their own style of appetizer: Italian antipasto, German vorspeise, Russian zakuska, Scandinavian smorgesbord, Spanish tapas, Greek orektika. ◼ When friends drop by unexpectedly, I step into the kitchen for a few minutes to mull a drink and toast some whole grain bread. I serve it with a wedge of cheddar cheese and some crisp green apples. At this time of year when appetites are flagging from too many chocolates and cream sauces, I find that my friends appreciate simple food.

One of the simplest things to serve surprise guests is cheese and crackers. Here are some classic combinations to serve with crackers or bread.

- Prosciutto and melon
- Pickled herring and sour cream
- Lox and cream cheese
- Cheddar cheese and apples
- Smoked oysters and sweet pickles
- Ham, cheese and pickles
- Sardines, tomatoes and Spanish onion slices
- Paper-thin sliced roast beef and horseradish
- Sardines, mustard and cheese
- Smoked salmon pieces, lemon juice, Spanish onion rings and capers on buttered black rye bread
- Fresh fruit with cottage cheese
- Cottage cheese and sour cream topped with sunflower seeds sautéed in oil or soy sauce
- Fresh mozzarella and sun-dried tomatoes with a drizzle of olive oil
- Salmon caviar and sliced eggs
- Sliced cold meat with dill pickle
- Hard-cooked eggs, apples and herring
- Smoked salmon topped with scrambled egg or sautéed mushrooms
- Corned beef or pastrami with horseradish or mustard
- Tomato, mayonnaise and grated cheese
- Sliced apples, carrots and mayonnaise
- Sliced roast beef, horseradish and pickle
- Sliced roast pork with applesauce and a sprinkle of cinnamon
- Kolbassa sausage and mustard

PLANNING YOUR EMERGENCY LARDER

Here are some ideas for starting a larder which will make it possible to please even the most demanding palate on short notice.

IN THE FREEZER

Home baking: cookies, fruitcakes, coffee cakes, pies, muffins

Quick baking ingredients: phyllo pastry, puff pastry, butter, nuts

Specialty breads: bagels, pita, rye, croissants, English muffins

Prepared foods: casseroles, homemade soup or soup stock, gravy, stews, hamburger patties and buns, pasta and sauce

Fruit and juices: apple cider for mulled cider, blueberries for blueberry muffins, cranberry juice for Christmas punch

Milk products: hard cheese, ice cream for milkshakes and sundaes

ON THE PANTRY SHELF

Canned fish and meat: salmon, tuna, sardines, anchovies, caviar, smoked fish, oysters

Jams, jellies, tinned fruit to spoon over ice cream

Candy, nuts, dried fruit and trail mix to sprinkle on yogurt

Beverages: canned juices, soda pop, mineral water

Condiments: mustard, ketchup, horseradish, pickles, relishes, cocoa or instant chocolate powder for hot chocolate, cinnamon for cinnamon toast, garlic for garlic bread

Crackers and packaged cookies

IN THE REFRIGERATOR

Cheeses: cheddar, flavored cream cheese, smoked cheese, cottage and ricotta for cooking

Smoked, salted, pickled meats and fish: salmon, mackerel, eels, herring, kippers, pastrami, ham, liverwurst, kolbassa, prosciutto

Fruit: mandarin oranges, grapes, pineapple, red and green apples, cranberries, lemons

Vegetables and herbs: for salads, serving raw with dips

Miscellaneous and staples: butter, eggs for eggnog, milk, light and heavy cream, sour cream, yogurt

FOR THE LIQUOR AND BEVERAGE CABINET

Liquor: light and heavy beer, gin, bourbon, rum, brandy, vodka, red and white wine

Other beverages: tea (regular and herbal), coffee (beans or ground, decaffeinated), apple cider, soda pop for mixing

Miscellaneous: honey, cinnamon sticks, whole cloves, whole nutmeg, ginger, whole allspice, cardamom pods

SEASONAL SPIRITS

SIMPLE EGGNOG

4	eggs, separated	4
¼ cup	white sugar OR icing sugar	50 mL
1 cup	light cream OR heavy cream	250 mL
½-1 cup	rum OR brandy	125-250 mL
1	whole nutmeg	1

In small bowl, beat egg whites until stiff. In large bowl, beat egg yolks and sugar until light yellow. Beat in liquor and gently fold egg whites into egg yolk mixture. Sprinkle with a grating of nutmeg.   **YIELD: 4 servings**

CHILDREN'S BLENDER EGGNOG (NON-ALCOHOLIC)

2	eggs	2
2 tbsp	white sugar	25 mL
¾ cup	light cream OR heavy cream	175 mL
¾ cup	milk	175 mL
1-2 tsp	vanilla	5-10 mL
⅛-¼ tsp	nutmeg	0.5-1 mL

Place eggs and sugar in blender. Process until light and frothy, about 30 seconds. Add cream, milk, vanilla and nutmeg. Process another minute and serve.   **YIELD: 2 to 3 servings**

SOUTHERN-STYLE EGGNOG

4	eggs, separated	4
1½ cups	heavy cream	375 mL
½ cup	icing sugar	125 mL
¼ cup	bourbon	50 mL
¼ cup	brandy	50 mL
1½ cups	light cream	375 mL
1	whole nutmeg	1

In a medium bowl, beat egg whites until stiff. In another medium bowl, whip heavy cream until thick. In a large bowl, beat egg yolks and sugar until light yellow. Beat in liquor and light cream. Gently fold egg whites and whipped cream into egg yolk mixture. Pour into punch bowl or individual glasses. Sprinkle with a grating of nutmeg.   **YIELD: 6 to 8 servings**

TIBETAN TEA

After a refreshing hike or any other outdoor activity, try this hot, rich and salty drink as a pick-me-up.

1 cup	boiling water	250 mL
1	tea bag	1
1 cup	milk	250 mL
1 tsp	butter	5 mL
	Pinch salt	
1 tsp	sour cream	5 mL

Bring water to a boil in small saucepan. Remove from heat and add tea bag. Cover and allow to steep 2 minutes. Remove and discard tea bag. Add milk, butter and salt and return almost to a boil. To serve, pour into 2 mugs and whisk in sour cream until frothy.   **YIELD: 2 servings**

HOT RUM TODDIES
FOR A CROWD

· ·

10 cups	water	2.5 L
3	2-in (5-cm) cinnamon sticks	3
6	whole cloves	6
12	whole allspice	12
10	whole cardamom pods	10
½ tsp	freshly grated nutmeg	2 mL
18 oz	rum	550 mL
¾ cup	honey	175 mL
6	lemons	6

In large stainless or enamel-coated saucepan, combine water and spices over high heat. Bring to a boil. Reduce heat and simmer, covered, 15 minutes. Remove from heat and strain liquids into large glass container. Discard spices. Cool liquid to room temperature and refrigerate until ready to heat and serve. To serve, reheat liquid to a boil. In each serving mug, place 1½ ounces (45 mL) rum, 1 tbsp (15 mL) honey, juice of ½ a lemon, and ¾ cup (175 mL) boiling hot liquid. Stir well.
YIELD: 12 servings

· ·

EGGNOG *(for various recipes,*
see pages 38, 39 and 194)

MULLED APPLE CIDER

· ·

1	apple	1
5	cloves	5
4 cups	apple juice OR hard cider	1 L
1	4-in (10-cm) cinnamon stick	1
½ tsp	ginger	2 mL
	White sugar to taste	

Stud apple with cloves and place in large saucepan with remaining ingredients over medium-low heat for ½ hour. Strain and serve hot.   **YIELD: 3-4 cups (750 mL-1 L)**

· ·

HOT MEAD

· ·

2	whole unpeeled oranges	2
¾ cup	honey	175 mL
1 cup	water	250 mL
1 cup	orange juice	250 mL
4	whole cloves	4
½ tsp	whole allspice	2 mL
1	5-in (12-cm) cinnamon stick	1
2 cups	vodka	500 mL

Leaving peel intact, slice oranges into rounds. Place all ingredients, except vodka, in medium saucepan over medium heat. Bring to a boil. Reduce heat, cover and simmer 30 minutes. Remove from heat, strain and return liquid to saucepan. Stir in vodka and return to low heat to keep warm for serving.
YIELD: 4 cups (1 L)

· ·

DUTCH BISHOP'S WINE OR MULLED WINE

This mulled wine is served on Saint Nicholas' Day (December 6) in the Netherlands. As Saint Nicholas was the Archbishop of Lycia, the drink served on his feast day was named for him.

1	**small orange**	1
4	**whole cloves**	4
4 cups	**red wine**	1 L
1	**1-in (2.5-cm) cinnamon stick**	1
1	**strip of lemon rind — ½ in (12 mm) wide and 3 in (7.5 cm) long**	1
	White sugar to taste	

Stud orange with cloves. Place in large stainless or enamel-coated saucepan with remaining ingredients on low heat for 20 to 30 minutes. Strain and serve hot. Mulled wine can also be made in a ceramic-lined crock pot.

YIELD: 3-4 cups (750 mL-1L)

QUICK TIDBITS AND APPETIZERS

· ·

POTTED CHEESE

· ·

Use any good strong-flavored cheese, such as old cheddar, in this recipe.

½ lb	cheese	250 g
½ cup	butter	125 mL
2 tbsp	brandy OR cognac OR sherry OR wine	25 mL
1 tsp	caraway seed	5 mL

Grate cheese into medium bowl. Cream butter and cheese and blend in alcohol and caraway seed. Pack in a jar or small crock. Cover and chill.   **YIELD: 1½ cups (375 mL)**

· ·

SMOKED SALMON *(see serving suggestion on page 35)*

HERRING SALAD

· ·

This dish is traditionally enjoyed in northern, eastern and central Europe on Christmas Eve and New Year's Eve. It can be a composed platter of tidbits or combined in a big bowl. Adjust the ingredients and amounts to suit your own taste or use the approximate amounts suggested. Many salad dressings work well with this dish. Several of them follow.

3	salt herring OR small bottle pickled herring (drained)	3
1 cup	cooked diced potatoes	250 mL
1 cup	cooked or canned diced beets	250 mL
2	chopped apples	2
½ cup	chopped dill pickles	125 mL
1	Spanish onion, cut in rings	1
3	chopped or quartered hard-cooked eggs	3
1 cup	chopped cold meat (veal, beef, tongue, pork, ham, lamb)	250 mL
2 tbsp	capers	25 mL
¼ cup	marinated mushrooms	50 mL
1	head lettuce	1

To prepare salt herring: rinse herring under running cold water. Place in large bowl and cover with water. Soak for a day, changing the water 2 or 3 more times. Drain well. Remove and discard head, tail, entrails and bones. Chop fish into small bite-size pieces. Place all salad ingredients in large serving bowl and toss lightly with dressing. Or, spread lettuce leaves on a large platter and arrange individual ingredients on leaves. Serve dressing in a separate cruet or bowl.

YIELD: 10 to 12 cups (2.5 to 3 L)

· ·

Honey Mustard Dressing

½ cup	salad oil	125 mL
1 tbsp	prepared mustard	15 mL
¼ cup	cider vinegar	50 mL
2 tbsp	honey	25 mL
	Salt and freshly ground black pepper to taste	

In small jar or bowl, beat together all ingredients or process in a blender.   **YIELD: ¾ cup (175 mL)**

· ·

Sweet Cream Dressing

1 cup	heavy cream	250 mL
1 tsp	prepared mustard	5 mL
1 tsp	sugar	5 mL
1 tbsp	vinegar	15 mL
½ tsp	dried dillweed (optional)	2 mL
	Salt and freshly ground black pepper to taste	

In small jar or bowl, beat together all ingredients or process in a blender.   **YIELD: 1 cup (250 mL)**

· ·

Sour Cream Dressing

1 cup	sour cream	250 mL
1 tsp	chopped green onion	5 mL
2 tbsp	freshly squeezed lemon juice	25 mL
	Salt and freshly ground black pepper to taste	

In small jar or bowl, beat together all ingredients or process in a blender.   **YIELD: 1 cup (250 mL)**

· ·

SPICY NUTS

. . . .

Toasted flavored nuts go great with cold beer. Use any of the spice combinations that follow and your choice of unsalted cashews, peanuts, almonds, pecans or walnuts.

2 tbsp	butter OR vegetable oil	25 mL
2 cups	nuts	500 mL
	Spice mixture	

Preheat oven to 300°F (150°C). In heavy skillet, warm butter or vegetable oil, and sauté nuts over medium-high heat for 2 to 3 minutes until light brown. In medium bowl, toss spice combination and hot nuts. Remove nuts to cookie sheet and toast 10 to 15 minutes stirring often, until nuts are drier and spices adhere.

Curry

1 tbsp	curry powder	15 mL
⅛ tsp	paprika	0.5 mL

Oriental

2 tbsp	soy sauce	25 mL
½ tsp	ginger	2 mL
½ tsp	garlic powder	2 mL

Salt and Pepper

1 tsp	salt	5 mL
½ tsp	freshly ground pepper	2 mL

Christmas

⅛ tsp	cinnamon	0.5 mL
⅛ tsp	cloves	0.5 mL
⅛ tsp	nutmeg	0.5 mL
2 tbsp	sugar	25 mL

YIELD: 2 cups (500 mL)

. . . .

GINGERBREAD HOUSE (see pages 81-89)

$\mathcal{T}$rue hospitality means adding water to the soup pot and pulling up another chair to the kitchen table. But I love all the flourishes of more formal entertaining, too. Once in a while it is fun to send out invitations, set out the best china on a good tablecloth with flowers and candles and cook up a storm. ◄ Half the fun of a party is in the planning, so I sit down with a cup of coffee and daydream. Do I want to invite a couple I'd like to know better for a cozy dinner of steamed clams and fresh pasta? Or am I in the mood for a fun night of noshes, wine and gossip with 15 or 20 noisy friends? Or because it is almost Christmas, is it time for a family brunch with cousins? Eight is about the maximum number of people to invite to a sit-down dinner party without extra help. ◄ I like to impress my guests with my culinary marvels, but more than that I like to sit down and visit with them. So I use recipes that are tried and true. Using company as guinea pigs can be very stressful. ◄ I try to visualize the logistics of the party and match the food with the mood. I imagine my friends arriving just as I am pulling crusty loaves of bread out of the oven. I hand them a glass of wine. They nibble on the bread and other appetizers in the living room, while I take care of details in the kitchen: adding fish to a broth or tossing a salad. ◄ Although it is not always possible, I try to avoid dishes that require a lot of concentration at the last minute such as whisking eight egg yolks into a

bourride. Cooking is all about timing, and my sense of timing disappears the instant one of my guests pops into the kitchen to chat. Allowing a breathing space between courses takes some of the pressure off the cook. Any dish that deflates or becomes soggy if not eaten instantly has no place at a dinner party without the help of servants.

. . . .

Planning a party on paper helps when the pressure is on. Here is a checklist of what I do.

1 Mentally sketch out the party.

2 Confirm date and time.

3 Invite guests by telephone or mail, at least two weeks ahead.

4 Decide on the whole menu including: appetizers, before-dinner drinks, soup, main course, hot side dishes, cold side dishes/salad, bread, sauces, salad dressings, relishes, condiments, mid-meal beverage, dessert, fruit/cheese/candy, after-dinner beverages (coffee, tea, liqueur).

5 Run through menu and make detailed lists of ingredients, and shopping lists separating things according to where and when they are to be purchased. Food staples, candies, alcohol and napkins can be bought weeks in advance. Specialty items such as delicatessen food, fish and flowers require last minute shopping.

A housekeeping checklist should be organized with the various jobs, who will do it and when, such as:

☐ scrub kitchen

☐ dust and vacuum living room

☐ dust and vacuum dining room

☐ scrub bathroom floor

☐ polish silverware

☐ iron tablecloths

6 Contemplate housekeeping chores. How will the house get clean? Where will people park and hang their coats? Make a checklist of cleaning chores and schedule when they will be done. Arrange for others to help if necessary.

7 Make a list of special cooking equipment, furniture and dishes needed to serve the meal. If they are to be borrowed, make arrangements for pickup and delivery.

8 Assess the menu and make a rough game plan for preparing it. What can be prepared in advance and safely stored in the refrigerator or freezer?

9 Get as much house cleaning, equipment picking up and grocery shopping done in advance as is humanly possible.

10 Post the menu in the kitchen. When things get harried, it may save the day.

11 If possible (sigh...) schedule an hour before guests arrive for a bath and a cat nap.

12 Keep a sense of humor and remember that the point of the whole exercise is to enjoy the guests.

PARTIAL MEALS AND SIMPLE MEALS

· ·

The problem at this time of year is not what to make for dinner, but what *not* to make. The magazines at the grocery checkout suggest we prepare five-course champagne brunches and multicourse dinners with expensive wines. The pressure is on.

In reality most of us are already burned out from lunch hours spent in department stores and evenings wrestling with pageant costumes. Putting on a little dinner party seems like a gargantuan task. Besides, we have probably already lost our appetites at a couple of work-related Christmas bashes. After a few cream-and-rum-sodden eggnogs, I could kiss the hostess who offers me a cup of clear lemon tea.

Sometimes we feel so overwhelmed from planning Christmas dinner that we decide not to bother doing any extra entertaining at all. But speaking as a sometime guest, I think that an invitation to a friend's house for cheese and crackers is infinitely better than no invitation at all. As much as I like good food, I prefer a relaxed time with simple fare to an evening with a kitchen-bound hostess who only appears to deliver the next chic course.

When it seems like too much trouble to have friends in, I figure I am overextending myself and it is time to check my priorities.

I invite my friends over and then try to figure out what to make. I look for something simple: a bowl of soup or a scrumptious dessert. I concentrate on doing my best at that one thing.

DROP IN FOR DESSERT

. . . .

Instead of the crowning glory that tops off a meal, dessert is often the last straw. A fine dessert should be appreciated with a good appetite and a steaming cup of hot coffee or tea.

I invite friends to drop in for dessert all year-round. But in winter we like soothing old-fashioned desserts like gingerbread or chocolate fudge pudding. It is a chance to rediscover never-fail desserts my mother depended on when I was growing up.

. . . .

ANY FOOL CAN MAKE THIS FOOL

A fool is a simple old-fashioned dessert made by folding fresh or stewed fruit — such as apricots, figs, dates or prunes — into whipped cream. It makes an ideal last-minute dessert.

1½ cups	chopped dried fruit	375 mL
1-1½ cups	apple juice	250-375 mL
¼ tsp	vanilla or almond extract OR	1 mL
2 tbsp	brandy or liqueur	25 mL
1 cup	heavy cream	250 mL
¼ cup	whole almonds	50 mL

In small saucepan, place dried fruit and 1 cup (250 mL) juice over low heat. Cover and simmer until fruit is soft, about 5 minutes, adding more juice if necessary. Cool, removing pits if any, and purée in blender or food processor. Add more juice if necessary to achieve a puréed, not paste texture. Remove to bowl and stir in flavoring or liquor. Whip cream until stiff and place in a serving dish. Fold in puréed fruit. Refrigerate until serving.

Preheat oven to 300°F (150°C). Wedge knife along seam of almonds to split them in half and toast on a cookie sheet until brown. Watch carefully because they burn easily. Cool and sprinkle toasted almonds on top just before serving.

YIELD: 4 to 6 servings

GINGERBREAD CAKE

This cake is delicious at any temperature. You can use plain or blackstrap molasses. Thanks to Marianna Thorbourne who has shared this recipe with hundreds of her students.

½ cup	butter	125 mL
½ cup	white sugar	125 mL
1	egg	1
½ cup	molasses (plain or blackstrap)	125 mL
1½ cups	white flour	375 mL
½ tsp	salt	2 mL
¾ tsp	baking soda	4 mL
½ tsp	cinnamon	2 mL
½ tsp	ginger	2 mL
½ cup	boiling water	125 mL

Preheat oven to 350°F (180°C). In large bowl, cream butter and sugar and beat in egg and molasses. In another bowl, sift together flour, salt, baking soda, cinnamon and ginger. Add flour mixture to butter mixture alternately with boiling water. Beat until well combined. Pour into buttered and floured 8-in (20-cm) square baking pan. Bake 35 to 40 minutes until a toothpick comes out dry and crumb-free. Serve as is, or with whipped cream, ice cream, custard, lemon sauce or with Vanilla Butter Sauce (recipe follows).
YIELD: 16, 2-in (5-cm) square servings

VANILLA BUTTER SAUCE

This tastes absolutely luscious melting down the sides of hot gingerbread.

1 tbsp	white flour	15 mL
½ cup	milk	125 mL
½ cup	white sugar	125 mL
½ cup	butter at room temperature	125 mL
1 tsp	vanilla	5 mL

In small saucepan, whisk together flour and milk until lump-free. Continue stirring over medium-low heat until thickened.

To microwave: combine in microwave safe bowl and cook in microwave on High for about 1 minute, stirring halfway through, until thickened.

Allow to cool *thoroughly*. Beat sugar, butter and vanilla into flour mixture with electric mixer until very light and fluffy. The texture can sometimes get curdlike, but the flavor is not altered. Serve over hot or cold gingerbread or hot plum pudding.
YIELD: about 1 cup (250 mL)

CRANBERRY
UPSIDE DOWN CAKE

. . . .

7 tbsp	butter, divided	95 mL
¼ cup	honey	50 mL
½ tsp	cinnamon	2 mL
¼ tsp	allspice	1 mL
2½ cups	fresh cranberries	625 mL
½ cup	white sugar	125 mL
1	egg	1
1½ cups	unsifted cake flour	375 mL
2 tsp	baking powder	10 mL
1 tsp	vanilla	5 mL
½ cup	orange juice	125 mL

Preheat oven to 375°F (190°C). In a small saucepan, melt ¼ cup (50 mL) butter and honey together over low heat. Stir in cinnamon and allspice. Pour into 8-in (20-cm) square cake pan. Add cranberries, stirring to coat evenly. In a large bowl, beat 3 tbsp (45 mL) butter and sugar until light. Beat in egg. Sift together flour and baking powder into small bowl. Stir vanilla into orange juice. Alternately beat flour mixture and orange juice into butter mixture. Continue beating for 1 minute. Pour over cranberries. Bake 30 minutes, until golden brown. Remove from oven, allow to sit 5 minutes and then invert on serving plate. Serve warm or cold with ice cream or whipped cream.   **YIELD: 12 servings**

. . . .

AN AFTER SKATING, SHOPPING, MOVIE OR CHRISTMAS CONCERT PARTY

After early evening activities are over, we are often too excited to go home to bed. I prolong the night by inviting friends over for coffee. It is a good way to entertain people too busy to commit themselves to a whole evening. It takes the pressure off me because it is impromptu and guests don't expect something fancy.

I make hot chocolate or hot fudge sundaes for the children and offer the adults herbal tea or coffee sometimes spiked with liqueur. Cinnamon toast is very easy to prepare; the combination of melted butter, sugar and cinnamon is magic.

COFFEE AND CHOCOLATE

I spread out the following ingredients on a table and friends help themselves:

- ◆ Hot coffee in a vacuum jug, percolator, dripolator or pot over a candle
- ◆ Whipped cream
- ◆ Grated semi-sweet chocolate
- ◆ Cinnamon sugar [¼ cup (50 mL) white sugar combined with 1 tsp (5 mL) cinnamon]
- ◆ Chocolate or coffee liqueurs
- ◆ Cinnamon sticks for stirring
- ◆ Mugs

MEXICAN BLENDER HOT CHOCOLATE

There's nothing simpler than adding chocolate mix to hot milk. But this traditional Mexican Christmas drink is extra thick and frothy, well worth the extra work.

4 cups	whole milk	1 L
4 oz	semi-sweet baking chocolate squares	125 g
½ tsp	cinnamon	2 mL
¼ cup	white sugar	50 mL
1 tsp	vanilla	5 mL
2	eggs	2

In large saucepan, scald milk over medium heat. Or heat in microwave in large microwave safe bowl. Do not boil. Coarsely chop chocolate and place in blender. Add cinnamon, sugar and 1 cup (250 mL) hot milk. Process 1 minute. With motor still running, add vanilla and eggs. Process until light brown and frothy. Pour blender contents back into saucepan with remaining milk and cook over low heat, stirring constantly until steam rises. Or return to microwave on High for 1½ minutes. Serve immediately.   **YIELD: 4 servings**

INCREDIBLE MICROWAVE
HOT FUDGE SAUCE

· ·

I keep some rock-hard vanilla ice cream in my freezer over the holidays. I can whip up this fudge sauce in the microwave and garnish it with nuts, candied fruit, chocolate mint sticks, even chopped candy canes. The taste is delicious, but what I especially like is that it turns thick and lumpy when it hits the ice cream.

¼ cup	melted butter	50 mL
½ cup	cocoa	125 mL
1¼ cups	brown sugar	300 mL
1 cup	heavy cream	250 mL
1 tsp	vanilla	5 mL

In an 8-cup (2-L) microwave safe bowl, combine all ingredients and microwave on High 3 to 4 minutes. Stir a few times, until thickened, and serve immediately.
YIELD: about 2 cups (500 mL)

· ·

AFTER WORK SOUP PARTY

Real soup does not come out of an envelope or can, and it certainly cannot be cooked in three minutes. While it can't be rushed, you don't have to stand over it all day either. It can be made one day and reheated the next. Other soups and chowders are quickly combined and eaten in less than an hour.

An invitation to share a bowl of soup with the cook is a real gift to a friend returning from a long day in a busy world.

TURKEY SOUP
WITH DILL DUMPLINGS

This nourishing soup made with fresh turkey backs, wings and legs has a rich turkey flavor. It's an economical meal in a bowl and everybody loves a dumpling. Make the broth the day before, add the dumplings and fresh vegetables an hour before you want to serve it.

3-4 lb	raw turkey parts	1.5-2 kg
2	medium onions	2
1	carrot, peeled	1
2	celery ribs	2
¼ cup	frozen peas	50 mL
	Salt and pepper to taste	

Dumplings

1 cup	white flour	250 mL
1½ tsp	baking powder	7 mL
¼ tsp	salt	1 mL
	Freshly ground pepper	
¼ tsp	dried dillweed	1 mL
2 tbsp	butter	25 mL
½ cup	milk	125 mL

In a large soup pot, place turkey and 1 whole peeled onion. Add enough water to completely cover turkey and bring to a boil. Reduce heat, cover and simmer until turkey falls off bones, at least 1 hour or more. Skim off and discard froth that rises to top. Remove turkey and onion to platter. Discard onion. When turkey is cool enough to handle, separate meat from bones, discarding bones. You can, at this point, chill broth to remove excess fat which congeals on top.

An hour before serving, finely chop second onion, carrot and celery. Add to soup. Simmer vegetables on medium-low while preparing dumplings. Sift flour, baking powder and salt into medium bowl. Stir in pepper and dillweed. Rub in butter until mixture resembles coarse meal. Gently stir in just enough milk to make a wet, sticky dough. Drop teaspoonfuls of dumpling dough on simmering soup. Cover and do not peek for 20 minutes. Lower heat if broth bubbles up. For a clearer soup, you may prefer to cook the dumplings separately in a medium saucepan of simmering hot water. When dumplings are cooked through, stir into soup. Add peas and cooled meat and allow to heat through before serving.   **YIELD: 10 servings**

LOBSTER OR CRAB CHOWDER

Because the lobster or crab is precooked, this simple recipe can be blended at the last minute. For richer flavor, substitute some fish broth or the water the crab or lobster is cooked in for some of the cream. You can use fresh, frozen or canned lobster or crab.

5	large potatoes, peeled and diced	5
¼ cup	butter	50 mL
1	large onion, finely chopped	1
2-3 cups	lobster OR crab meat	500-750 mL
6 cups	light cream	1.5 L
	Salt and pepper to taste	

Precook potatoes until almost cooked through. In large soup pot, melt butter and sauté onion until transparent. Add precooked lobster or crab meat and continue sautéeing 2 or 3 more minutes. Add cream, potatoes, salt and pepper and increase heat to medium. Do not allow to boil. Serve with fresh rolls. **YIELD: 8 to 10 servings**

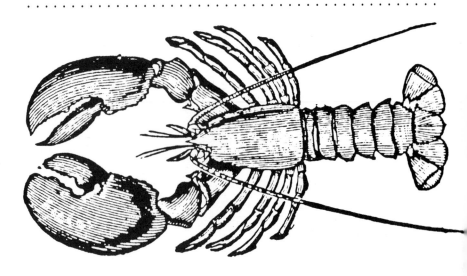

DAYTIME PARTIES

The Christmas season is a time when the wheels of daily routine grind to a halt. Children who are usually lockstepped into school, homework and lessons are suddenly sprung into a 10-day limbo. Add lots of sugar, Santa hype and parents with their own deadlines and expectations, and there is a potential for disaster. On the other hand, there is time for dad to get down on the floor and play Monopoly all day and time for mom to help make a sock puppet.

All year long my children quietly put up with grown-up company. When adults are over for an evening, they hardly get a word in edgewise. Sometimes they retreat to the television set or, much to their disgust, are put to bed early.

But Christmas is family time and the children are let in on the fun of our parties. They help with every aspect of them from invitations to planning the menu. They often come up with waffles or pancakes as a main course and fresh fruit, which they love, especially zipper-skinned mandarin oranges which are imported only at Christmas time. Other old standbys are roast chicken, noodles and chocolate cake. After the meal, we plan an activity that includes everyone: a walk, a slide down the hill, a board game or a story.

FAMILY WAFFLE OR PANCAKE BRUNCH

Waffles or Pancakes: With a combination of several of the following toppings: whipped butter, maple or corn syrup, honey, whipped cream, cherry or blueberry sauce, grated chocolate, fruit yogurt, honey or sweet lemon butter, plate of icing sugar with a spiral of lemon wedges, applesauce, toasted coconut or nuts, granola.

OR Baked Cottage Cheese Pie *(see recipe page 70).*

Platter of Fresh and Canned Fruit: Bananas, mandarin oranges,

Honey or Jam Butter
Make sweet butter using ¼ cup (50 mL) butter at room temperature and ½ cup (125 mL) of your favorite honey, jam or marmalade. Beat them together until light and fluffy and spoon over hot pancakes or waffles. Yield: about ½ cup (125 mL).

grapes and fresh pineapple are all popular with the children.

Bacon, Sausage or Ham: Before company arrives, broil or fry it until not quite done and place it in a warm oven to keep warm.

Juice and Milk: Children especially like individual paper packs or cans with straws.

Tea and Coffee or Irish Coffee: The grownups deserve a special treat too.

Fluffy Lemon Butter
This tangy butter calls for ¼ cup (50 mL) soft butter along with ½ cup (125 mL) icing sugar and 1 tsp (5 mL) finely grated lemon rind. Beat ingredients until fluffy and spoon over hot pancakes, waffles or toast.
Yield: about ½ cup (125 mL).

. . . .

WAFFLES FOR A CROWD
. . . .

If possible, bring the waffle iron to the table so your company can enjoy the cooking process too.

6	eggs, separated	6
2½ cups	white flour	625 mL
2 cups	whole wheat flour	500 mL
2 tbsp	baking powder	25 mL
½ tsp	salt	2 mL
3 tbsp	white sugar	45 mL
¾ cup	vegetable oil OR melted butter	175 mL
4½-5 cups	milk	1.125-1.25 L
1 tbsp	vanilla	15 mL

Season and preheat waffle iron according to manufacturer's instructions. In large bowl, beat egg whites until stiff. Sift flour, baking powder, salt and sugar into a medium bowl. In another large bowl, whisk together egg yolks, oil or melted butter, 4½ cups (1.125 L) milk and vanilla. Just before waffles are to be cooked, gently stir flour mixture into egg mixture, leaving lumps. Fold in egg whites. Add more milk if necessary to make a batter the texture of chili. When waffle iron is hot, pour batter into center of iron until three-quarters of surface is covered. Close lid and wait until steam stops, 3 to 5 minutes. Carefully remove waffles and serve immediately. Close lid and allow iron to heat up to temperature again before adding more batter.
YIELD: about 2 dozen

. . . .

PANCAKES FOR A CROWD

4	eggs, separated	4
2 cups	white flour	500 mL
1 cup	whole wheat flour	250 mL
1½ tbsp	baking powder	22 mL
½ tsp	salt	2 mL
2 tbsp	white sugar	25 mL
½ cup	vegetable oil OR melted butter	125 mL
4 cups	milk	1 L
1 tbsp	vanilla	15 mL

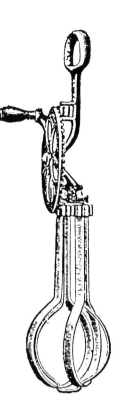

Season and preheat flat griddle or frying pan over medium heat. In small bowl, beat egg whites until stiff. In medium bowl, sift together flour, baking powder, salt and sugar. In large bowl, beat egg yolks, vegetable oil or melted butter, milk and vanilla. Gently stir flour mixture into egg mixture leaving lumps. Do not overbeat. Fold in egg whites. Drop ¼ cup (50 mL) of batter onto medium-hot griddle. When bottom is light brown and bubble holes have formed on surface, flip pancakes onto other side. Continue frying briefly to brown other side. Serve immediately. **YIELD: 48 pancakes**

MICROWAVE BLUEBERRY
OR CHERRY SAUCE

. . . .

The microwave is excellent for reconstituting frozen berries. They stay whole and plump rather than falling apart when cooked on top of the stove.

2 cups	**unsweetened frozen blueberries OR cherries**	500 mL
2-4 tbsp	**white sugar**	25-60 mL
1 tbsp	**cornstarch**	15 mL
	Cinnamon (optional)	

In a 4-cup (1-L) microwave safe bowl, stir together sugar and cornstarch. Stir in blueberries or cherries and cinnamon, if desired. Cover with plastic wrap and cook on High 4 to 7 minutes, stirring occasionally, until slightly thickened. Fruit will gel more as it cools.   **YIELD: 2 cups (500 mL)**

. . . .

STOVE TOP BLUEBERRY
OR CHERRY SAUCE

. . . .

¼ cup	**white sugar**	50 mL
1¼ tbsp	**cornstarch**	20 mL
1 cup	**apple juice**	250 mL
2 cups	**frozen unsweetened blueberries OR cherries**	500 mL
	Cinnamon (optional)	

In medium-size heavy saucepan, combine sugar and cornstarch. Whisk in apple juice. Cook over medium-low heat, stirring constantly until thickened. Add blueberries or cherries, and cinnamon if desired, and gently heat through.
YIELD: 2 cups (500 mL)

. . . .

IRISH COFFEE

Omit the sugar in this if you're using sweetened liqueur.

1-2 tbsp	**Irish whiskey OR brandy OR coffee liqueur**	15-25 mL
1 tsp	**white sugar**	5 mL
1 cup	**strong, hot coffee**	250 mL
	Heavy cream	

Place Irish whiskey, brandy or coffee liqueur and sugar in warmed mug or heatproof wine glass. Fill with coffee and top with cream, whipped if you prefer, to taste.
YIELD: 1 cup (250 mL)

"Refreshing"

BAKED COTTAGE CHEESE PIE

Children love this dish. Serve it with sour cream or yogurt, maple syrup and/or fruit. If cooking for a crowd, make up two or three pans separately; do not double or triple the recipe.

1 cup	white flour	250 mL
½ cup	whole wheat flour	125 mL
1 tsp	baking powder	5 mL
⅓ cup	butter	75 mL
2	eggs	2
¾ cup	milk	175 mL
4 cups	creamed cottage cheese	1 L
½ tsp	dried dillweed	2 mL
1 tbsp	grated onion	15 mL
	Freshly ground pepper to taste	

Preheat oven to 350°F (180°C). Into medium bowl, sift flours and baking powder. Rub in butter until it resembles coarse meal. In small bowl, beat eggs and milk together. Stir into flour mixture. Pour one third of mixture into buttered 6 × 10 in or 8 × 8 in (20 cm) pan or casserole with high sides. In another medium bowl, combine cottage cheese, dillweed, onion and pepper. Pour cheese mixture into pan and top with remaining egg and flour mixture. Bake 50 to 60 minutes, until light brown and bubbly. Allow to cool 5 minutes before cutting in squares. **YIELD: 4 servings**

COFFEE KLATCHES AND TEA PARTIES

· ·

If hosting a tea party is not your cup of tea, then how about a coffee klatch? While a tea party sounds ever so civilized, a *klatsch* (the German word for "gossip") sounds like a more down-to-earth affair. Whatever the style, a relaxed afternoon with friends has become a luxury for most people in the work force.

Feeling nostalgic for my mother's tea parties and following the instructions in her old cookbook, I once tried to reproduce the little bitty sandwiches (egg salad and chopped olives, cream cheese roll-ups with sweet pickle centers) I remembered from my childhood. They tasted fine but they didn't look tempting. I discovered there is an art to these fussy little things, and they require the same amount of concentration as the tiny tarts I remember my mother filling with lemon custard.

A tea party menu can be as formal or sophisticated as you like — the traditional tea and cucumber sandwiches or wine and caviar, pickled shrimp and buffalo milk cheese.

I am better at coffee parties, throwing a pecan bundt cake in the oven and serving a decent cup of coffee. For more substance I add a big chunk of Jarlsberg cheese and some sweet seedless grapes. Whatever the style, it is a wonderful way to entertain friends morning or afternoon.

· ·

PECAN COFFEE CAKE
. . . .

Most recipe boxes contain a variation on this classic nut and cinnamon coffee cake. Just in case you don't have one, here is a delicious version.

1 cup	butter	250 mL
1¾ cups	white sugar	425 mL
4	eggs	4
2½-2¾ cups	white flour	625-675 mL
2 tsp	baking powder	10 mL
1 cup	milk	250 mL

Streusel

¾ cup	brown sugar	175 mL
2 tsp	cinnamon	10 mL
½ tsp	allspice	2 mL
¼ cup	flour	50 mL
¼ cup	melted butter	50 mL
1 cup	chopped pecans	250 mL

Preheat oven to 350°F (180°C). In a large bowl, cream butter and white sugar and beat in eggs. In a separate bowl, sift together flour and baking powder. Beat flour mixture into butter mixture alternately with milk. In a small bowl, combine streusel ingredients. Pour half the cake batter into buttered and floured bundt pan. Top with half the streusel mixture. Top with remaining batter and top with remaining streusel. Bake 45 minutes to 1 hour, until a toothpick comes out dry and crumb-free. Remove cake from oven. Allow to cool 5 minutes and invert on cooling rack. When cool, remove to serving platter and wrap well until serving.   **YIELD: 1 large cake**

. . . .

SUGAR-GLAZED HAM (see page 77)

Here are a few hints for organizing a buffet party with children:

☐ Forget social obligations at this special time of year. Invite only people you feel comfortable with: your best friends and people you would like to get to know better.

☐ Anticipate the group dynamics — where will people sit, circulate? Where will the children be — upstairs or all over the house?

☐ Do you want to plan it around any outside activities — skating on the back pond, a barbecue, a bonfire or tobogganing?

☐ Plan something for the children to do — a treasure hunt, a sing-along, games like 'Murder in the Dark,' charades or a memory game. Don't let them languish in front of the television.

BUFFET PARTIES

It may seem mad to plan a party for 26 when the guest list includes 12 adults, 12 children and a couple of babies. But a few times a year we throw caution to the wind and have a real gang over. I grew up in the midst of a large extended family and I miss the inter-generational celebrations we used to have, the special foods, the chaos and fun. For my own children, I miss that confident, unselfconscious feeling of belonging. So I do my best to re-create these parties in another way — with friends.

The secret to this kind of entertaining is obviously in the planning. We invite a fair number of children but also an equal number of grownups so that things never get totally out of hand. There are always a few people who don't like standing around. They feel most comfortable holding the

baby or helping with the food. I happily put them to work chopping last minute vegetables, carving roasts or serving tea.

It helps to be optimistic. I set everything up . . . and then just let it happen. After the first guest steps in the door, things are out of my control anyway.

SAMPLE MENU

. . . .

This meal is basically a sandwich but the quality of all the ingredients makes it special. The choices of fresh vegetables and garnishes allow for different tastes. The lamb is marinated and roasted with the ham early in the day. It is sliced very thinly and laid out just before guests arrive. Bread and sauces are freshly made or purchased and laid out on platters at the last minute.

Marinated Roast Leg of Lamb (page 76)
Roast ham or Sugar-Glazed Ham (page 77)
Fresh pita bread or buns
Garnishes: mayonnaise, Tzatziki (page 78), Homemade Sweet Butter (page 79), and Honey Mustard (page 79)
Fillings: diced tomatoes, shredded lettuce, bean sprouts, sliced Spanish onion, diced green, red and yellow pepper and sliced fresh mushrooms
Potato chips
Chocolate chip cupcakes
Wine, beer, juice packs with straws

. . . .

☐ Plan a simple menu that appeals to all ages and limit the choices.

☐ Plan a menu that is easy to dispense — cookies or cupcakes instead of a cake, which requires plates and forks. Or serve ice cream in a cone to avoid the bowls and spoons.

☐ Provide lots of heavy-duty paper serviettes.

☐ Feed the children first, with the help of adults.

☐ Lay out the food on the table in the easiest order for people to fill their plates.

MARINATED ROAST LEG OF LAMB

2	cloves garlic	2
¼ cup	olive oil	50 mL
¼ cup	herb vinegar	50 mL
1 tsp	rosemary	5 mL
1 tsp	thyme	5 mL
1 tsp	freshly ground pepper	5 mL
1 tsp	soya sauce	5 mL
4-6 lb	leg of lamb	2-3 kg

Crush garlic. Combine garlic and remaining ingredients, except lamb, in shallow glass or ceramic dish, large enough to hold lamb. Place lamb in dish and spoon marinade over it. Cover lightly with waxed paper. Refrigerate for 4 to 6 hours, basting a few times. Preheat oven to 325°F (160°C). Place lamb in roasting pan and roast about 30 minutes per pound or until meat reaches an internal temperature of 160°F (71°C) for rare meat or 180°F (82°C) for well-done meat. Baste several times with pan juices.
YIELD: 10 to 12 small servings

SUGAR-GLAZED HAM

This is always a great alternative to fowl during the holidays. Red and green cherries as decoration give it a seasonal touch.

4-5 lbs	smoked ham	2-2.5 kg
2 tsp	whole cloves	10 mL
1 cup	whole pineapple rings	250 mL
¼ cup	glacéed red and green cherry halves	50 mL
½ cup	packed brown sugar	125 mL
½ tsp	Dijon mustard	2 mL
2 tbsp	pineapple juice	25 mL

Preheat oven to 325°F (160°C). With a sharp knife, score fat on ham in crisscross pattern. Press cloves into cross marks. Decorate with pineapple and cherries. Mix sugar, mustard and pineapple juice and brush over ham. Bake 20 min/lb (40 min/kg), about 1½ to 1¾ hours. Baste with pan juices 2 or 3 times. **YIELD: 6 to 8 servings.**

TZATZIKI (YOGURT DIP)

1	large cucumber	1
¼ tsp	salt	1 mL
1½ cups	plain whole milk yogurt	375 mL
1	garlic clove, minced	1
1 tsp	herb vinegar	5 mL
1 tbsp	snipped fresh dillweed OR	15 mL
1 tsp	dried dillweed	5 mL
	Freshly ground pepper to taste	
	Fresh mint leaves for garnish	

Peel cucumber and remove seeds. Grate flesh into small bowl and sprinkle with salt. Place a saucer and some kind of weight over grated cucumber and set aside 15 minutes. Press saucer and pour off liquid. Place cucumber in strainer and continue to squeeze out excess liquid. Return cucumber to clean bowl and stir in remaining ingredients. Refrigerate for at least 2 hours before serving.   **YIELD: about 2 cups (500 mL)**

HOMEMADE SWEET BUTTER

2 cups	32% heavy cream	500 mL

Pour cream into food processor fitted with plastic blade. Process for 2 to 3 minutes, until butter curds separate from buttermilk. Pour off liquid and save to add to baking if you like. Knead butter to remove excess liquid. Pat into small crock or bowl with cover.   **YIELD: 1 cup (250 mL)**

HONEY MUSTARD

This really enhances the flavor of glazed ham.

¼ cup	honey	50 mL
⅓ cup	vegetable oil	75 mL
¼ cup	prepared OR Dijon mustard	50 mL
2 tsp	dry mustard powder	10 mL
2 tbsp	vinegar	25 mL
½ tsp	dried thyme OR dill	2 mL

In a small bowl, beat all ingredients together until thick and creamy.   **YIELD: about 1 cup (250 mL)**

CHOCOLATE-CHIP CUPCAKES

1 cup	white flour	250 mL
¼ cup	cocoa	50 mL
1 tsp	baking soda	5 mL
½ cup	white sugar	125 mL
1	egg	1
1 tsp	vanilla	5 mL
1 cup	applesauce	250 mL
⅓ cup	melted butter	75 mL
⅔ cup	chocolate chips	150 mL
18	cherry-filled chocolates (optional)	18

Preheat oven to 350°F (180°C). In a large bowl, sift together flour, cocoa, baking soda and sugar. In a small bowl, beat together egg, vanilla, applesauce and melted butter. Stir egg mixture and chocolate chips into flour mixture all at once, until well combined. Pour batter into large paper cups in muffin tins, three-quarters full. Bake 20 to 25 minutes, until a toothpick comes out dry and crumb-free. Remove from oven and, while still warm, swirl top of cupcakes in Chocolate Glaze (recipe follows). Cool and serve. Top with cherry-filled chocolates if desired.   **YIELD: 18**

CHOCOLATE GLAZE

1 cup	icing sugar	250 mL
2 tbsp	cocoa	25 mL
2 tbsp	corn syrup	25 mL
2 tbsp	very hot water	25 mL
1 tbsp	vegetable oil	15 mL

In small bowl, combine all ingredients and mix well.
YIELD: ¾ cup (175 mL)

THEME PARTIES

. . . .

GINGERBREAD HOUSE PARTY

. . . .

A gingerbread man that survives the rolling, cutting and baking process with all its limbs intact is a rare thing indeed. Constructing a complete residence for the two-dimensional beings is definitely a Herculean task. But every Christmas I am smitten by the glossy photographs of Hansel and Gretel gingerbread cottages in the magazines.

The first time we built a gingerbread house at our place, we were four grown adults with a leisurely afternoon ahead of us. On our team was a graduate engineer and a finishing carpenter. Both had built full-scale houses. As back up we had a Boeuf Bourguignonne simmering on the stove and an uncapped bottle of Southern Comfort. In as few as five hours, we had a decent little house complete with an annex, stained glass windows and icicles dribbling all over it. It didn't look like the pictures in the magazines, but it was a respectable little house.

Years later, we built a gingerbread house, with the *help* of four children. While the adults had construction experience, the childrens' lack of it neutralized the benefit of their expertise. There was a tense four-hour period when two adults slaved away at rolling, cutting, baking and gluing the thing together. Nerves were on edge as the edges of the house failed to stick. We saved the day with an electric drill and toothpick nails and gobs of icing to fudge over the rough edges.

Then, with the help of a mountain of candy and the children, who are the real candy experts, the fun began. Ecstatic little conversations could be heard about the virtues of plastering a wall in Smarties versus jelly berries.

Gingerbread house building can be a fun activity to share with family and friends. Here are a few hints on how to have a successful party.

1 Mix the dough and the icing glue the day before the party and wrap it well.

2   Take a whole day off to devote to the construction of the house, without the children. They get invited to the fun, decorating part.

3   Use a simple pattern for your first endeavour (such as the pattern included here) or design the house and sketch it on paper. Transfer your pattern onto cardboard and cut it out.

4   Assemble all necessary tools and roll out the dough to an even thickness on cookie sheets. Place the pattern pieces on the dough and cut away the excess with a sharp knife.

5   Cut out the windows and fill them to the top with crushed Lifesavers (or any hard sugar candy) which will melt into clear sugar windows.

6   Place the cookie sheets one at a time into the oven, for perfect browning.

7   Follow the instructions for gluing the pieces together.

8   Stay calm and don't worry if the roof looks like it might leak.

9   For the party, plan on cooking something easy like chili or stew, that guests can serve themselves. Don't worry about a dessert. Everyone loves to sample the candy.

. . . .

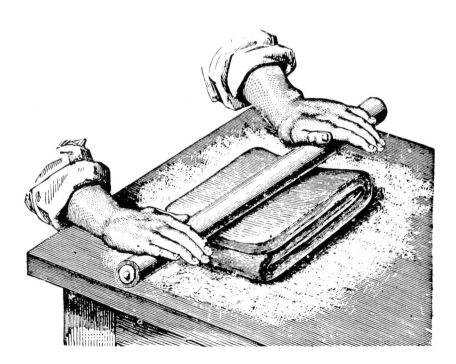

EQUIPMENT NEEDED

To make a pattern

Paper pattern for house of your design or from this book

Tracing paper
Pencil
Scissors
Cardboard
Ruler

If making your own house design, sketch it on tracing paper, using a ruler and pencil. Draw the end wall, side wall, half the roof, additional doors, shutters or dormers if desired.

If using pattern in book, place tracing paper on pattern and copy lines with pencil. Cut out pattern pieces in tracing paper. Place tracing paper pieces on cardboard. Trace around edges with pencil. Carefully cut out cardboard pattern pieces.

To make the walls and roof pieces

1 batch Gingerbread House Dough (recipe follows)
Cookie sheets
Aluminum foil
Butter
Flour
Rolling pin
Knives
Ruler
Egg flippers
Wire cooling racks

Preheat oven to 325°F (160°C). Line cookie sheets with aluminum foil. Butter and lightly flour foil. With lightly floured rolling pin, roll out dough on cookie sheet to a thickness of ¼ in (6 mm). Using prepared paper pattern or drawing freehand, cut design into dough with knife and ruler. Carefully remove excess pieces. Bake 15 to 20 minutes until slightly firm. Remove from oven; cool long enough to handle. Carefully peel off aluminum foil and allow cookie pieces to cool completely on cooling rack.

To assemble the house

Plywood base or equivalent
Cooled gingerbread pieces
1 batch Icing Glue (recipe follows)
Unopened cans for propping up walls while they dry
Electric drill and toothpick nails (optional)

The icing glue bonds well, but it takes a while to dry. Ways must be found to hold the pieces together. Experiment by propping the sides up with tins of food, or leaning them against heavy books. It is difficult to give exact instructions but improvise with what you have on hand.

Start by spreading a generous bead of icing on the base where the house will stand. Ice the bottom edges of one end wall and one side wall. Ice the perpendicular edges where they come together. Press the edges together at a 90-degree angle and place them on the iced base. Hold them in place by propping them up until semi-dry enough to add the other walls.

The roof is more difficult and may require more than one set of hands to ease it into place. Start by spreading a generous bead of icing to join the two main roof pieces. Allow it to dry well before gluing it to the top of the walls.

To decorate

Batch Icing Glue (recipe follows)
Lots of candies and store-bought cookies — all shapes and sizes (licorice allsorts shingles, candy cane pillars, chocolate rosebud flowers)
Toothpicks for spreading

Spread a little icing on the back of each candy or cookie and press into place. Prevent unused portion of icing from drying out by covering it with plastic wrap or damp towel.

. . . .

GINGERBREAD HOUSE DOUGH

1 cup	butter	250 mL
1¾ cups	brown sugar	425 mL
1¼ cups	white sugar	300 mL
2 tbsp	molasses	25 mL
6	eggs	6
6 cups	white flour	1.5 L
2 tsp	baking soda	10 mL
1 tbsp	ginger	15 mL
1 tbsp	cinnamon	15 mL
1 tbsp	allspice	15 mL

In a large bowl, cream butter and sugars. Beat in molasses and eggs. In another large bowl, sift dry ingredients. Combine mixtures and knead into smooth ball.

ICING GLUE

3	egg whites	3
1½ tsp	cream of tartar	7 mL
3-3½ cups	icing sugar	750-875 mL

In a large bowl, beat egg whites and cream of tartar until stiff but not dry. Gradually add icing sugar, beating for about 5 minutes until it reaches spreading consistency. If too dry, add a few drops of water. Cover with plastic wrap or damp towel when not using, to prevent drying out.

SIMPLE ALTERNATIVES TO BUILDING A LARGE GINGERBREAD HOUSE

1 Make several small houses for children to decorate individually. They can combine them to make a Christmas village.

2 Cut out the design of a flat two-dimensional gingerbread house. Paint the perspective with icing and decorate with candy and cookies.

3 Cut out 6 in (15 cm) disks of gingerbread. After baking and cooling, decorate them, mosaic-style, with candies to make wall plaques. Drill a small hole, before baking, through the top. Later, run some yarn through it for hanging up.

4 Make smaller disks or other cookie cutter shapes with holes for tree ornaments. Decorate with candy and/or icing. They can be hung as soon as the icing dries (an hour or two).

GINGERBREAD HOUSE PATTERN

The easiest thing to use for a template is stiff cardboard that is able to be cut by scissors or a knife easily. Work to scale and draw out your grid on the cardboard. Each square of the grid represents 1 inch (2.5 cm). There are templates for:

◆ base
◆ roof — two pieces
◆ front wall
◆ back wall
◆ end walls — two pieces
◆ side walls
◆ four wall supports
◆ four chimney sections

NOTE: Remember the slabs must be cut while they are warm and soft since they will harden as they cool. Assemble the house on a bread board or cookie sheet for easy turning.

BASE

ROOF

SIDE WALL

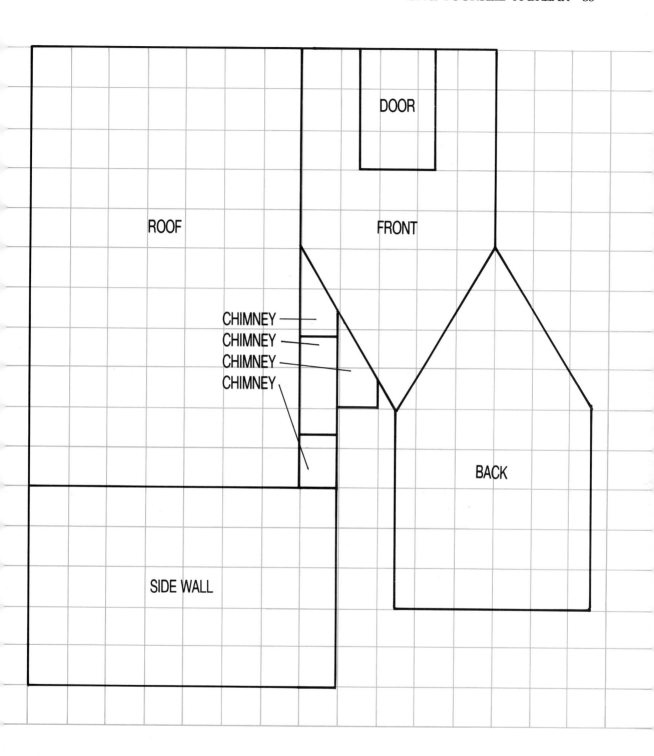

ROOF

FRONT

DOOR

CHIMNEY

CHIMNEY

CHIMNEY

CHIMNEY

BACK

SIDE WALL

MARZIPAN PARTY

. . . .

At traditional pre-Christmas parties in Denmark, guests are given a small amount of colored marzipan to mold into fruit, vegetable and animal miniatures. Prizes are awarded for the best creations.

. . . .

MARZIPAN CREATURES

. . . .

According to an old Danish legend, no Christmas visitor is allowed to leave the house without taking a bag of Christmas cookies. Otherwise the host and hostess run the risk of the holiday guests carrying the Christmas Spirit away in their empty hands.

Almond paste can be made by grinding equal amounts of blanched almonds and sugar together in a food processor; not a difficult but a tedious task. Therefore we recommend purchasing the almond paste.

1	egg white	1
1 cup	almond paste	250 mL
1-1½ cups	icing sugar	250-375 mL
½-1 tsp	lemon juice	2-5 mL

You also need:
Food dyes
White sugar
Decorations such as whole cloves (for fruit stems), cocoa, chocolate sprinkles, silver balls, raisins, colored sugar crystals and poppy seeds
Tools for molding and poking such as toothpicks, forks and knives

In a large bowl, beat egg white until fluffy. Mash and beat in almond paste. Beat in 1 cup (250 mL) of icing sugar. Knead in more icing sugar and lemon juice to achieve a soft modelling clay consistency. Divide dough into as many pieces as you like and knead in food dye. You can protect your hands by using waxed paper or plastic wrap. Or you may prefer to roll natural colored marzipan in colored sugar crystals. To color sugar, stir a few drops of food dye into a small amount of white sugar. Dry in a microwave oven on Medium for a few minutes or in a regular oven at 400°F (200°C) for about 5 minutes, stirring a few times. Shape into miniatures.

Suggested shapes
Pink: pigs
Orange: oranges, peaches, apricots, carrots
Yellow and brown: bananas, pears, chicks
Natural: lambs, mushrooms, potatoes rolled in cocoa dirt
Red: apples, hearts, strawberries, tomatoes
Green: leaves, Christmas wreaths, turtles
Cocoa brown: beavers, bird's nest with colored eggs

Try rolling shapes in colored sugar; poking them with tooth-picks; and experimenting with various textures.

. . . .

POT LUCK AND PITCH-IN PARTIES

. . . .

Back when I was in high school, a bunch of us would spend New Year's Eve cooking together. One of our parents would graciously let us in the kitchen and vacate the house for the evening. Now that I am grown up and have children, I can appreciate how very gracious they were.

The excitement started a few days before New Year's when we planned the menu. We were very inexperienced. In fact we cooked only once a year, but we were up for anything. Twenty years later I still remember every detail of one meal we considered very gourmet: Guacamole, Boeuf Bourguignonne, Caesar Salad and Strawberries Romanoff.

The afternoon of December 31 was spent at the grocery store. At eight o'clock that evening, we assembled and swung into action. We chopped and stirred and tasted. We argued and acted foolish. At about eleven o'clock we sat down to dinner in the formal dining room and felt very grown up.

I don't really remember how things tasted, but it all seemed wonderful. Today, I invite friends over to my house in the spirit of those times to share the joy of preparing and eating meals. Not only do we have a good time together, but I don't have to do all the work. The process of cooking the meal is part of the evening's entertainment.

. . . .

POT LUCK

. . . .

I enjoy fancy parties, but even more, I enjoy unpressured cooking and spontaneous entertaining.

My idea of a perfect winter dinner goes something like this. I wake up Saturday morning to a snowy kind of day and so there is no point in going outside to battle the elements. I get an uncontrollable urge to bake bread. While the bread is rising, I poke around in the refrigerator and find a ham bone from last night's supper. I put a pea soup on to simmer. While it's bubbling away, I decide to transform a few slightly withered apples into a bowl of fragrant applesauce.

Five minutes to six and there is a knock at the door — friends I've been meaning to call for months. They wander into the kitchen where the combined aroma of freshly baked bread, soup and apples makes it impossible for them to refuse my dinner invitation. They help me set the table and do the dishes later. In the meantime, we've had the most relaxed time catching up on each other's news.

This kind of relaxed entertaining is wonderful. But it takes luck to bring uninvited guests and a pot of homemade soup together at just the right moment.

A pot luck is a good way to make spontaneous parties happen. It ensures that the guests will show up, but the host or hostess is not responsible for every detail. The menu, the guest list, even the time can be open-ended.

One New Year's Day we had an open house pot luck party. A month before, we dashed off 70 photocopied letters inviting people to come to our house January 1 "noonish and all afternoonish." We asked them to bring their families and friends and something to eat. There were no R.S.V.P.s, so we did not know who was going to show up or what they were going to bring. We supplied the party with a basic time frame and a space to happen. We provided a large table with empty plates, cutlery, serviettes, and something to drink (juice, beer and mulled wine).

Friends came and went in waves from twelve noon to eight o'clock. They brought with them the best of their kitchens and the table groaned with food. There was a fine spread of courses from appetizers to desserts. Although we did have some basic host responsibilities such as hanging up coats, offering drinks and laying out food, we had the best time we've ever had at one of our own parties. We almost felt like guests.

The simplest pot luck involves inviting a bunch of friends to come over and to bring something to eat. To ensure a balance of courses, make a chart like this. Fill in each person's name and what they are contributing. People who don't cook or are very busy can bring a bottle of wine, a hunk of cheese or some bakery rolls.

Theme (if any)

Number of guests

Appetizers

Main dishes

Side dishes/Salads

Breads

Beverages

Desserts

POT LUCK IDEAS
. . . .

To avoid gastronomical juxtapositions, here are some ways to co-ordinate the meal.

Pot luck with a theme

Invite all guests to bring a dish from a particular ethnic tradition — Italian, Creole or South American — or a favorite dish from childhood. There is a place even for tuna casserole with potato chip topping.

No dishes meal

Ask guests to bring appetizers and other finger foods. Finicky little rollups and other tasty tidbits are fun to make when they are the only thing you're making; and cleanup is simplified.

Sandwich fillings

The host provides fresh bread — pita, egg, rye, onion buns, crusty rolls, brioche, bagels, heavy wholewheat — mayonnaise and quality mustard. Guests bring sandwich fillings.

Salad pot luck

Host supplies bread, beverage and dessert. Friends bring various kinds of salads:

    raw vegetable salad
    cooked vegetable salad
    fruit salad
    meat or poultry salad
    fish or shellfish salad
    egg or cheese salad
    pasta or grain salad

Oil and Vinegar Dressing for Vegetables
Use white, herb, wine, balsamic, raspberry or any one of your favorite vinegars.
In a bottle or bowl, combine and mix well: ½ cup (125 mL) quality olive oil, ¼ cup (50 mL) fresh lemon juice or vinegar and salt and freshly ground pepper to taste.
Yield: ¾ cup (175 mL)

. . . .

SALADS
. . . .

These are really appreciated this time of year. Here is a list of fruits and vegetables usually available which make good winter salads.

Vegetables

Artichokes	Kale
Avocadoes	Leeks
Beans	Lettuces: romaine, Boston,
Broccoli	Bibb, iceberg
Brussels sprouts	Mushrooms
Cabbage	Onions
Cauliflower	Parsley
Celeriac	Peas (flat snow)
Celery	Peppers: red, green, yellow
Chayote	Potatoes
Chicory	Radishes
Chinese cabbage	Rutabaga
Cucumber	Spinach
Endive	Squash, winter and summer
Escarole	Sweet potatoes
Fennel	Turnips
Jerusalem artichokes	

Fruits

Apples	Oranges
Bananas	Papayas
Coconuts	Pears
Cranberries	Persimmons
Grapefruit	Pineapples
Grapes	Pomegranates
Kiwi fruit	Tangelos
Lemons	Tangerines
Limes	
Kumquats	
Mandarins	

Dried Fruits and Nuts

Almonds	Pears
Apples	Pecans
Apricots	Pistachio nuts
Dates	Prunes
Figs	Raisins
Filberts or hazelnuts	Walnuts
Macadamia nuts	

· ·

ROASTED CHESTNUTS

Nurturing chestnuts over glowing coals is a lot of work, but when the furry husks are peeled off and you savor the sweet chewy flesh, you'll agree it's worth it for this once-a-year delicacy. Whatever the cooking source, cut a ½-in (1-cm) crisscross into the flat side of each chestnut. This will allow the steam to escape and prevent the nuts from exploding all over the place. I speak from experience!

Open Fire

If you don't own a special chestnut-roasting pan, improvise with a wire mesh popcorn popper or an aluminum pie plate with holes poked in it. Place scored chestnuts in pan over the hot coals, shaking occasionally. Depending on the intensity of the fire, chestnuts may take up to 20 minutes to cook to a soft and chewy texture.

Electric or Gas Oven

Place scored chestnuts on cookie sheet and bake at 450°F (230°C) for 10 to 20 minutes, stirring occasionally until the texture is soft and chewy. Peel and eat them as soon as they are cool enough to handle.

Frying Pan

If you have a wood stove, get a good hot fire going, place a heavy cast iron skillet on the top and add some scored chestnuts. Stir occasionally until the texture is soft and chewy.

Microwave Oven

Place scored chestnuts in a circle on a microwave safe plate. Because cooking time in the microwave depends on volume, it is hard to be exact in these instructions. Cook on High power until steam rises from nuts and the crisscross puffs open.

ROASTED CHESTNUTS (see above)

A WINTER DINNER AROUND THE FIREPLACE

. . . .

Friends walk in the door, stamp the snow off their feet and we hand them hot toddies. All the ingredients for supper are set out in the living room and everyone cooks. We rescue potatoes from the fire, roast marinated mushrooms and beef tidbits on skewers, tear off hunks of melted cheese and fresh bread.

MENU

Melted cheese with fresh braided egg or crusty bread
Marinated roasted mushrooms and scallops
Marinated lamb and/or beef tidbits
Baked potatoes with toppings
Fresh vegetable and fruit platter (cherry tomatoes, carrot sticks, apples, pears, grapes)
Iced strawberry yogurt or lemon ice
Roasted chestnuts

. . . .

MELTED CHEESE

. . . .

Wonderful textural changes take place when cheese is set next to a hot fire. The edge closest to the heat becomes soft and gooey. It is scraped off and eaten immediately with fresh bread or baked potatoes. The cheese and bread flavors provide a nice contrast to spicy marinated food. Use a firm mild cheese such as Raclette, Jarlsberg, Emmentaler or Gruyère.

---

2 lb	chunk firm mild cheese	1 kg

Wrap top and sides of a thick wooden cutting board with aluminum foil. Place it on bricks close to the coals. Place cheese on board and, as it melts, scrape off and serve on bread or crackers. The time it takes to melt varies with temperature of fire, distance from fire and variety of cheese. It may take 30 minutes to begin to soften.   **YIELD: 2 lb (1 kg)**

. . . .

BAKED POTATOES

Bake potatoes in a regular oven until they are almost cooked through. Rub a little butter into the skin, wrap them in a double layer of foil and place them on the hot coals. They must be watched carefully.

MARINATED ROASTED MUSHROOMS AND SCALLOPS

Combine everything in a jar and let it sit overnight. The garlicky, slightly smoky, moist taste of the scallops is one of the best things I have ever eaten. Use fresh thyme, dill or basil for the herbs in this if possible.

½ cup	quality olive oil	125 mL
¼ cup	wine vinegar OR lemon juice	50 mL
1 tbsp	fresh parsley	15 mL
1 tbsp	fresh herbs OR	15 mL
1 tsp	dried herbs	5 mL
½ tsp	salt	2 mL
½ tsp	freshly ground pepper	2 mL
1	large clove garlic, minced	1
1 lb	fresh scallops	500 g
1 lb	large fresh mushrooms	500 g

In a large wide-mouth jar or non-metallic bowl, combine olive oil, vinegar or lemon juice, parsley, herbs, salt, pepper and garlic. Add scallops, stirring to coat with marinade. Wipe mushrooms clean (do not wash) and add to olive oil mixture. Stir to coat with marinade. Marinate 4 to 24 hours in refrigerator, stirring occasionally. Place on skewers and roast over coals in fireplace or barbecue until brown.
YIELD: 4 to 6 servings (more if appetizers)

Garnishes for Baked Potatoes
□ Butter, sour cream, yogurt or tzatziki, green onions or chives.
□ Coarsely diced soft vegetables, raw or marinated in simple oil and vinegar dressing are delicious! Try any combination of avocadoes, tomatoes, green, yellow or red peppers, olives, onions or hot peppers.
□ Grated cheese or Melted Cheese, or chopped bacon, mushrooms and onions.
□ Finely diced, crunchy vegetables, raw or marinated in simple oil and vinegar dressing are also good. Try any combination of carrots, celery, turnip, kohlrabi, broccoli, cauliflower and onions.

MARINATED BEEF TIDBITS

. . . .

Use a tender cut of boneless beef for this dish.

1 lb	beef	500 g
2 tbsp	peanut oil	25 mL
2 tbsp	wine vinegar	25 mL
2 tbsp	soy sauce	25 mL
2 tbsp	honey	25 mL
1	clove garlic, crushed	1
½ tsp	ginger	2 mL
½ tsp	cinnamon	2 mL
½ tsp	freshly ground pepper	2 mL

Cut beef into bite-sized pieces large enough to stay on skewer over fire. In bottom of plastic or glass bowl, combine remaining ingredients. Add beef, tossing to cover. Refrigerate 1 hour before roasting. Place on skewers and roast over hot coals until cooked to individual taste. **YIELD: 4 to 6 servings (more if appetizers)**

. . . .

MARINATED LAMB TIDBITS

. . . .

Parsley, rosemary and thyme are the best herbs to use in this recipe.

1 lb	boneless lamb	500 g
¼ cup	olive oil	50 mL
2 tbsp	herb vinegar	25 mL
1	clove garlic, crushed	1
2 tbsp	fresh herbs	25 mL
2 tsp	dried herbs	10 mL
½ tsp	freshly ground pepper	2 mL
½ tsp	salt	2 mL
	OR	
1 tbsp	soy sauce	15 mL

Follow instructions for Marinated Beef Tidbits. **YIELD: 4 to 6 servings (more if appetizers)**

. . . .

SCOTTISH SHORTBREAD *(see pages 13-16)*

CHAPTER 4

CHRISTMAS
BAKING

PREPARING FESTIVE FOODS

*I*n our country community *the* question, at this time of year, is: "Have you got your Christmas baking done yet?" The standard around here includes: buttery shortbread decorated with bits of cherry and candied peel, sugar cookie bells or stars decorated with silver balls and colored sugar crystals, rum balls rolled in chocolate sprinkles, nut crescents dredged in icing sugar, fruitcake fingers, Nanaimo bars and gumdrop or cherry poundcake. ⬛ Because I am never at the point in my baking where I expect I should be, I usually answer the question with a self-denigrating, "Are you kidding?" But the combined weight of all the "should be" things — making balsam fir wreaths, hand dipping candles, sewing smocked pinafores, shopping, entertaining — can be over-whelming. ⬛ There is simply no way to do all the baking that our full-time homemaker grandmothers did. To cope, I force myself to make choices, weighing the time, money and the energy required to do each activity. I love good food more than a clean house. My house will be filled with the fragrant aroma of braided fruit breads, but the kitchen floor will be sticky with crumbs. I like my children to be part of the Christmas fun more than I like beautifully wrapped presents. So I let them wrap. ⬛ When friends stop by during the Christmas season, I like to offer them a cup of coffee and some fresh baking — a cardamom bun or a gingerbread man with its arms missing and a mouth where its necktie should be — served proudly by my assistant bakers, my children.

COOKIES

Cookies are as much a part of Christmas as stockings and carols. At Christmas we take the time to dig deep into the recipe box and pull out old favorites, the ones with all the warm childhood associations.

To make life easier, I have collected recipes over the years that give the best results for the least amount of hassle.

I pat out and bake large sun-shaped slabs of Scottish short-bread in half the time it takes to cut out bell and star-shaped sugar cookies.

I whip together refrigerator dough and make five different kinds from a single batch, getting the most amount of variety with the least amount of effort. I also roll the dough in waxed paper and store it in the refrigerator. Then, when friends drop by, it is easy to slice and bake a few cookies and serve them hot out of the oven.

Hand-shaped kourabiedes are easier to make than rolled and cut zimsterne. But squares and bars which are pressed into a pan and cut en masse are even easier. Cookies dropped from the end of a spoon are just as easy. After a day at work I may not have the energy to struggle with spritz cookie presses, springerle rolling pins and krumkake irons, but I can usually summon up enough strength to throw some squares into a pan.

Finding a place for the flood of cookies hot off the press also takes planning. I like cookie tins the best and scrounge them whenever I can. Aluminum or waxed paper layers keep the cookies intact. Many people freeze cookies in batches in tins or on their sides on plastic tomato trays. About a week before Christmas, the cookies are removed from the freezer and an assortment is placed on serving plates. These are re-wrapped and placed back in the freezer. An hour before serving they are unearthed and ready for company.

EASY COOKIES

EMMA AND MOM'S CHOCOLATE DROPS

These cookies are doubly easy because they don't have to be baked. That's why four-year-old Emma Slipp and her Mom make them.

2 oz	unsweetened chocolate squares	55 g
½ cup	butter	125 mL
¾ cup	white sugar	175 mL
½ cup	milk	125 mL
1 tsp	vanilla	5 mL
1 cup	grated coconut	250 mL
2 cups	rolled oats	500 mL

In medium saucepan, cook chocolate, butter, sugar and milk over medium-high heat. Bring to a boil for 2 to 3 minutes, stirring occasionally. Remove from heat and stir in vanilla, coconut and oats. Drop spoonfuls on cookie sheets covered with aluminum foil or waxed paper. Set aside to harden. If you have anxious tasters helping you, put the cookies outside in the cold to cool.   **YIELD: 3 to 4 dozen**

JIMMY'S MERINGUES

Canon Herbert Puxley, a gentleman in his eighties, and a friend of our family, fondly remembers his Christmases in England as a boy. During the season, at Avebury, the family home, he would play golf with his sister Sal and munch on meringues made from this recipe.

2	egg whites	2
⅛ tsp	cream of tartar	0.5 mL
½ cup	white sugar	125 mL
12-14	whole blanched almonds	12-14

Preheat oven to 225°F (110°C). In medium bowl, beat egg whites and cream of tartar together until light and foamy. Add sugar, 1 tbsp (15 mL) at a time, until all is added and mixture is stiff. Line cookie sheets with aluminum foil, drop dough onto sheets at least 1 in (2.5 cm) apart. Press an almond into the center of each meringue and bake 50 minutes. Cool slightly and peel cookies off foil to cool on wire rack.   **YIELD: 12 to 14 cookies**

Options: make larger meringues and serve as a dessert with whipped cream, custard or chocolate sauce.

ITALIAN AMARETTI OR ALMOND MACAROONS

2	egg whites	2
½ tsp	vanilla	2 mL
½ tsp	almond extract	2 mL
1½ cups	finely ground almonds	375 mL
2½ cups	icing sugar	625 mL

Preheat oven to 325°F (160°C). In large bowl, beat eggs until stiff. Gently fold in vanilla, almond extract, almonds and 2 cups (500 mL) icing sugar. Line cookie sheets with aluminum foil and drop spoonfuls of batter on foil, at least 1 in (2.5 cm) apart. Sift remaining icing sugar over cookies. Set aside in cool place, to dry for a few hours. Bake 20 to 25 minutes until light brown. Cool slightly and peel cookies off foil to cool on wire rack.   **YIELD: 2½ dozen**

ICEBOX COOKIES

. . . .

These are as easy to shape as drop cookies — just slice them off the roll. The dough is wrapped in foil and refrigerated so it's easy to take slices off the roll and bake fresh cookies for company.

The basic cookie is a light butter cookie. With a double batch, you can make several variations.

¾ cup	butter	175 mL
¾ cup	white sugar	175 mL
1	egg	1
1 tsp	vanilla	5 mL
2 cups	white flour	500 mL
2 tsp	baking powder	10 mL

In a large bowl, cream butter and sugar and beat in egg and vanilla. In another bowl, sift together flour and baking powder. Add to butter mixture and stir until well combined. Form dough into 2 rolls of 1½ in (3.75 cm) in diameter and 8 in (20 cm) long by patting it onto waxed paper, plastic wrap or foil. Lift, roll and smooth to form even cylinders. Wrap, pinching ends and chill in refrigerator at least 1 hour, until hard enough to slice. To bake, preheat oven to 350°F (180°C). Remove roll from refrigerator. Unwrap and cut into ¼-in (6-mm) slices. To retain the round shape, rotate the roll as you cut. Place on buttered cookie sheets and bake 10 to 12 minutes, until edges are light brown.   **YIELD: 5 dozen**

PINWHEELS

Roll dough out between 2 layers of waxed paper to form a rectangle 6 × 10 in (15 × 25 cm). Remove top layer of waxed paper and spread on: ⅓ cup (75 mL) jam, marmalade, nuts, stewed fruit (such as apricots or dates), cinnamon (or any other spices) and sugar. Then re-roll dough into a cylinder and refrigerate.

Variations

CHERRY NUT COOKIES
Add to the basic dough:

½ cup	minced nuts	125 mL
½ cup	minced red and green candied cherries	125 mL

CHOCOLATE COOKIES
Knead in, for a pretty marbled effect:

¼ cup	cocoa	50 mL

NUT OR COCONUT COOKIES
Roll the raw dough roll to coat the outside in:

⅓ cup	finely chopped nuts OR toasted coconut	75 mL

JAM, MARMALADE OR MAPLE CREAM GLAZE
Spread warm cookies with:

⅓ cup	jam OR marmalade OR maple cream	75 mL

LEMON ICING GLAZE

⅓ cup	icing sugar	75 mL
1 tbsp	lemon juice	15 mL
	colored sugar (optional)	

Combine ingredients, spread over warm cookies and sprinkle
with colored sugar, if desired.

. . . .

HAND-SHAPED COOKIES

· ·

KOURABIEDES

· ·

These Greek butter cookies, dredged in icing sugar, are served year-round, but at Christmas a clove is inserted into each cookie to recall the gifts of the Wise Men to the Christ child. The pliable dough can be shaped into crescents, horseshoes or alphabet letters.

1 cup	butter	250 mL
¼ cup	sifted icing sugar	50 mL
1	egg	1
1 tbsp	brandy	15 mL
1 tsp	vanilla	5 mL
1 cup	finely ground almonds	250 mL
1½-2 cups	white flour	375-500 mL
	Whole cloves	
½ cup	icing sugar	125 mL

Preheat oven to 325°F (160°C). In medium bowl, beat together butter and icing sugar until light and fluffy, about 5 minutes. Beat in egg, brandy and vanilla until well mixed. Stir in almonds and knead in enough flour to form a soft dough. Shape cookies by hand into flat domes, crescents or logs. Press a clove into each cookie. Bake on ungreased cookie sheets 20 to 25 minutes until tawny colored, but not brown. Remove to cooling rack. Cool and dust generously with icing sugar before storing between layers of aluminum foil or waxed paper in cookie box or tin. **YIELD: 3 dozen**

· ·

KERSTKRANS or DUTCH CHRISTMAS WREATH
(see page 110)

KERSTKRANS AND BANKETLETTER

Fill puff pastry with a marzipan filling and shape it into a Dutch Christmas wreath or traditional alphabet-shaped pastries.

13 oz	frozen puff pastry	379 g
1	egg	1
1-2	egg whites	1-2
½ cup	white sugar	125 mL
1 tsp	almond extract	5 mL
1 tsp	grated lemon rind	5 mL
1½ cups	finely ground almonds	375 mL

Glaze

¼ cup	apricot jam	50 mL
3-4 tsp	freshly squeezed lemon juice	15-20 mL
¼ cup	icing sugar	50 mL
¼ cup	candied peel and cherries	50 mL

Defrost puff pastry at room temperature so that it is soft but still cool. In medium bowl, beat egg whites until stiff. Beat in white sugar, almond extract and lemon rind. Stir in ground almonds.

To make large wreath: Roll pastry to form a rectangle 25 × 5 in (63.5 × 12.5 cm). Evenly distribute filling down center of pastry. Pinch edges closed, using a little water to help the seal if necessary. Form into a large circle, pinching ends together.

To make letters: Roll pastry to form a rectangle 25 × 5 in (63.5 × 12.5 cm). Cut lengthwise into 2 strips, each 2½ in (6.4 cm) wide. Evenly distribute filling down center of 2 strips. Pinch edges closed, using a little water to help the seal if necessary. Cut each strip in half. Form into 4 alphabet letters.

Place wreath or letters seam-side down on buttered cookie sheet. Set aside in warm spot for 30 minutes. Preheat oven to 425°F (220°C). Brush with beaten egg and bake 35 to 40 minutes until crisp and brown. With spatula, loosen pastry from cookie sheet but allow to remain on sheet while you glaze and cool them.

Glaze: In small saucepan, combine apricot jam and 1 tsp (5 mL) lemon juice. Place over low heat, just long enough to melt it. Brush jam over top of wreath. In a cup, combine icing sugar and 2 to 3 tsp (10 to 15 mL) lemon juice. Drizzle over wreath. Decorate with peel and cherries.   **YIELD: 1 wreath or 4 letters**

FRUIT CUTOFFS

This cookie is somewhere between a hand-molded and a bar cookie. Ropes of dough are baked and cut into bars while still warm out of the oven. They are quick and easy to make.

¾ cup	butter	175 mL
½ cup	white sugar	125 mL
1 tsp	vanilla	5 mL
2 cups	white flour	500 mL
½ cup	jam OR stewed fruit OR cranberry sauce	125 mL

Glaze

½ cup	icing sugar	125 mL
2-3 tsp	lemon juice	10-15 mL

Preheat oven to 350°F (180°C). In large bowl, cream butter, sugar and vanilla. Add flour, kneading until well combined. Form into 4 ropes, 12 in (30 cm) long. Cover cookie sheets with aluminum foil. Butter foil and place ropes on sheets. With fingers make a channel down the center of each rope. Fill channel with jam, stewed fruit or cranberry sauce. Bake 15 to 20 minutes until bottom is light brown. In cup, combine icing sugar and enough lemon juice to make a paste. Drizzle glaze on cookies. While still warm, cut diagonally to form bars about ¾ in (20 mm) wide.   **YIELD: about 40 bars**

DUTCH PEPERNOTEN

On December 5 in Holland, the door bell rings and the excited children assemble at the door. A mysterious black hand tosses Pepernoten or peppernuts through the opened door. The hand that tosses the treats is said to belong to St. Nicholas's Moorish helper, Black Peter.

2 cups	white flour	500 mL
¼ tsp	baking powder	1 mL
¼ tsp	cinnamon	1 mL
¼ tsp	nutmeg	1 mL
¼ tsp	cloves	1 mL
½ cup	brown sugar	125 mL
⅛ tsp	finely ground black pepper	0.5 mL
2	egg yolks	2
1 tbsp	corn syrup	15 mL

Preheat oven to 350°F (180°C). Into large bowl, sift flour, baking powder, cinnamon, nutmeg and cloves. Stir in brown sugar and pepper. In small bowl, whisk together egg yolks and corn syrup. Add to flour mixture and knead well into smooth ball. If mixture is crumbly, add more corn syrup. Form into small ½-in (1-cm) balls. Place on oiled cookie sheets and make a slight indentation with finger. Bake 20 to 25 minutes until dry and hard.   **YIELD: 4 to 5 dozen**

SUGAR COOKIES

A friend asked me to find a cookie recipe that was childproof. She wanted a dough that could be mixed, rolled and cut out easily by little hands, without frustration and tears. She wanted a cookie that was tasty enough to warrant all the work. This recipe is a terrific one to make with children.

¾ cup	butter	175 mL
1 cup	white sugar	250 mL
2	eggs	2
1 tsp	vanilla	5 mL
2½ cups	white flour	625 mL
1 tsp	baking powder	5 mL
½ tsp	salt	2 mL

Preheat oven to 375°F (190°C). In large bowl, cream butter and sugar and beat in eggs and vanilla until light. Into small bowl, sift together flour, baking powder and salt. Add flour mixture to butter mixture, kneading to form a ball. Wrap with plastic and chill at least 1 hour. Roll out on a lightly floured surface to a thickness of ¼ in (63 mm). Cut into shapes with lightly floured cookie cutters. Remove with spatula to ungreased cookie sheets. Decorate with Glaze for Sugar Cookies (recipe follows) or press in chocolate sprinkles, candied fruit bits, raisins, chocolate chips, gumdrops, nuts or colored sugar crystals (combination of white sugar and a drop of food dye). Bake 8 to 10 minutes, until edges are light brown. Remove to cooling racks. Pipe on any butter icing, if desired, when cool.

GLAZE FOR SUGAR COOKIES

My daughters, Anna and Ruthie, love to paint colored designs on unbaked cookies. They cover their cookies with a plain white base and add drops of different colors. While baking, the colors meld, giving a pretty enamelled effect.

1 cup	icing sugar	250 mL
2 tbsp	lemon extract OR vanilla	25 mL
	Few drops water	
	Few drops food dyes	

Prepare cookies and place on cookie sheets. In small bowl, blend sugar and lemon extract or vanilla and enough water to form a thick paste. Divide into 3 or more small bowls, leaving 1 batch uncolored. Stir different colored food dyes into each bowl. Use toothpicks to paint designs on cookies. Bake as directed. **YIELD: 4 dozen, 2½-in (6.3-cm) cookies**

SQUARES AND BARS
. . . .
TWO SQUARES IN ONE
. . . .

This easy square starts with a rich shortbread base on which you can build any topping. I put two toppings in one pan for more variety. Use jam, puréed fruit or bits and pieces left over from other baking projects.

Base

½ cup	butter	125 mL
¼ cup	brown sugar	50 mL
1 cup	white flour	250 mL
1 tsp	vanilla	5 mL

Toppings

FRUIT
Use a combination of candied peel, glacéed fruit and raisins.

½ cup	fruit	125 mL
¼ cup	chopped walnuts	50 mL
3 tbsp	corn syrup	50 mL

CINNAMON NUT

½ cup	chopped walnuts OR pecans	125 mL
3 tbsp	brown sugar	50 mL
¼ tsp	cinnamon	1 mL
3 tbsp	corn syrup	50 mL

Preheat oven to 350°F (180°C). In medium bowl, cream butter and brown sugar together. Knead in flour and vanilla to form a ball. Pat into an 8-in (20-cm) square pan. Combine fruit and cinnamon nut toppings in separate bowls. Sprinkle half of

cookie base with fruit topping, the other half with cinnamon nut topping. Bake 25 to 35 minutes until cookie base is firm. Cut into squares or bars with sharp knife while still warm. Allow topping to set before removing from pan.
YIELD: 64, 1-in (2.5-cm) squares

. . . .
NUT SQUARES
. . . .

Base

½ cup	rolled oats	125 mL
¼ cup	brown sugar	50 mL
1 cup	white flour	250 mL
½ cup	melted butter	125 mL
1 tsp	vanilla	5 mL

Topping

3	eggs	3
¾ cup	corn syrup	175 mL
1 cup	chopped pecans OR walnuts	250 mL

Preheat oven to 350°F (180°C). In large bowl, combine rolled oats, brown sugar and flour. Stir in butter and vanilla. Pat into buttered 8-in (20-cm) square pan. Bake 15 minutes. Meanwhile, in a medium bowl, beat eggs and corn syrup together. Stir in nuts. Remove baked base from oven and spread on topping. Return to oven and continue baking 30 minutes, until puffed and brown. Allow to cool slightly before cutting bars.
YIELD: 64, 1-in (2.5-cm) squares

. . . .

CHOCOLATE-CHIP NUT BARS

Base

½ cup	brown sugar	125 mL
½ cup	butter	125 mL
2 cups	white flour	500 mL
1 tsp	vanilla	5 mL

Topping

1 cup	finely chopped pecans	250 mL
½ cup	butter	125 mL
¼ cup	brown sugar	50 mL
1 cup	chocolate chips	250 mL

Preheat oven to 350°F (180°C). In large bowl, cream brown sugar and butter. Add flour, until well combined. Pat into 9 × 13-in (22.5 × 33-cm) pan. Top with pecans. In small saucepan, melt butter and brown sugar over medium heat. Bring to a boil for 1 minute, stirring constantly. Pour over pecans, spreading evenly with back of spoon. Bake about 15 minutes, until bubbly. Remove from oven and sprinkle chocolate chips evenly over top. Cool 10 minutes and cut while still warm.

YIELD: about 40 bars

LAST-MINUTE CAKES

Here are a few delicious spice and dried fruit cakes that don't need to be aged. In fact we usually start nibbling on them hot out of the oven.

LAST-MINUTE FRUIT CAKE

This moist, golden cake leans towards the cakey side. It can also be doused with brandy and aged like any other fruit cake.

½ cup	butter	125 mL
½ cup	white sugar	125 mL
3	eggs	3
2 tbsp	orange OR apple juice	25 mL
1 tsp	vanilla	5 mL
1 cup	white flour	250 mL
1 tsp	baking powder	5 mL
½ tsp	cinnamon (optional)	2 mL
½ tsp	nutmeg (optional)	2 mL
1 cup	candied peel	250 mL
1 cup	golden raisins	250 mL
1 cup	finely chopped nuts	250 mL
2 tbsp	or more, brandy (optional)	25 mL

Preheat oven to 300°F (150°C). In a large bowl, cream butter and sugar. Beat in eggs, juice and vanilla. In a medium bowl, sift flour, baking powder, and cinnamon and nutmeg, if desired. Stir in candied peel, raisins and nuts. Blend flour mixture into butter mixture. Pour into 4 × 8 in (10 × 20 cm) loaf pan lined with buttered waxed paper. Fold waxed paper over top. Bake 1½ hours until light brown and a toothpick inserted in the middle will come out dry and crumb-free.   **YIELD: 1 cake**

DUNDEE CAKE

. . . .

Jean Macpherson, who grew up in Scotland, makes this fruit cake for her family every year. It is traditionally made in a round pan, decorated with split almonds and served with tea, of course.

¾ cup	butter	175 mL
¾ cup	white sugar	175 mL
3	small eggs	3
1½ cups	white flour	375 mL
1½ tsp	baking powder	7 mL
	Pinch salt	
½ cup	dark raisins	125 mL
½ cup	golden raisins	125 mL
½ cup	currants	125 mL
½ cup	chopped candied peel	125 mL
¼ cup	slivered almonds	50 mL

Preheat oven to 300°F (150°C). In large bowl, cream butter and sugar. Beat in eggs 1 at a time with a sprinkle of the flour. Into medium bowl, sift remaining flour and baking powder. Dredge dark raisins, golden raisins, currants and candied peel in mixture. Stir flour mixture into butter mixture. If mixture seems too stiff, add 1 tbsp (15 mL) water. Pour into 8-in (20-cm) square, round or springform pan that has been lined with buttered or waxed paper. Scatter almonds on top or arrange in a design. Bake 1½ to 2 hours, until a toothpick comes out dry and crumb-free. Allow cake to cool for a few minutes in pan. Remove to cooling rack. Peel off paper and cool completely before wrapping well in plastic wrap. **YIELD: 1 cake**

. . . .

CANDIES

· ∗ · · · · · · · · · · · · · · · · ·

My friend Susan Hower has a yellowing scrap of paper on which is typed a recipe for 'Grandma Tody's Pecan Rolls.' Every Christmas, Susan's grandmother, Irene Devor Jacobi, prepared opera creams, dipped them in caramel and rolled them in chopped pecans. She made 13 rolls, one for each of her grandchildren. In 1958 she typed up the recipe, affixed a Christmas seal of two elves at the top and mailed a carbon copy to each grandchild. Susan has never found a commercial pecan roll that comes even close to her grandmother's. Unfortunately, I found the recipe too difficult to reproduce here.

Today, however, unlike when Grandma Tody was a girl, a whole world of tantalizing candy is imported to our doorsteps: Italian nougat, barley sugar toys, candy canes and Belgian chocolate. Because candy making can be finicky and the results expensively disastrous, we don't often attempt to make it at home. But the taste of good homemade candy is worth the risk. We have included only those recipes which are easy and can be made without a lot of special equipment beyond a candy thermometer.

· ∗ · · · · · · · · · · · ·

FRESH COCONUT MEXICAN FUDGE

2 cups	white sugar	500 mL
1 cup	heavy cream	250 mL
¾ cup	freshly grated coconut	175 mL

In medium saucepan, combine sugar and cream over medium-high heat. Stir occasionally until mixture comes to a boil. Reduce heat to medium and cook undisturbed until mixture reaches the soft ball stage (240°F/115°C) on a candy thermometer. Remove from heat and stir in coconut. Beat until mixture thickens. To form candy, drop teaspoonfuls onto aluminum foil.   **YIELD: 16 candies**

CHOCOLATE MARSHMALLOW ROLL

4 oz	unsweetened chocolate squares	125 g
½ cup	butter	125 mL
25	large marshmallows	25
2	eggs	2
¾ cup	icing sugar	175 mL
½ cup	walnuts	125 mL
1 cup	grated coconut	250 mL

In small saucepan, melt chocolate and butter together over low heat or in microwave. Cool slightly. Cut marshmallows into quarters. In large bowl, beat eggs and icing sugar. Stir in walnuts, marshmallow pieces and melted chocolate mixture. With hands, form into two cylinders, 2 in (5 cm) in diameter and 9 in (22.5 cm) long. Roll in coconut. Roll in waxed paper or aluminum foil. Refrigerate overnight, slice and serve.
YIELD: 36 pieces

EASY FUDGE

. . . .

This is easily made in a microwave or a saucepan on the stove top. The chocolate is already sweetened and the sugar is in solution in the condensed milk. It is softer than regular fudge and must be refrigerated.

⅓ cup	butter	75 mL
8 oz	semi-sweet baking chocolate squares	250 g
½ cup	coarsely chopped walnuts OR pecans	125 mL
1 tsp	vanilla	5 mL
10 oz	tinned sweetened condensed milk	300 mL
½ cup	coarsely chopped candied cherries OR pineapple	125 mL

In medium saucepan, melt together butter and chocolate over low heat. Add remaining ingredients and continue cooking and stirring until smooth.

To microwave: Place butter and chocolate in medium microwave safe bowl. Microwave on medium for 2 to 3 minutes until melted, stirring a few times. Stir in remaining ingredients and microwave on medium for a few more minutes. Beat until smooth.

Pour into buttered 8-in (20-cm) square pan. Refrigerate at least 3 hours to set. Cut into 1-in (2.5-cm) squares.   **YIELD: 64 pieces**

. . . .

SIMPLEST TRUFFLES

Chocolate and cream — what a combination! You can use any one of your favorite liqueurs for flavor.

2 cups	semi-sweet chocolate chips	500 mL
1 cup	heavy cream	250 mL
2 tbsp	liqueur	25 mL
1 tsp	vanilla	5 mL
¼ cup	cocoa OR chocolate sprinkles	50 mL
¼ cup	icing sugar	50 mL
¼ cup	finely chopped nuts	50 mL

In medium bowl, place chocolate chips. Pour cream into small saucepan over medium-high heat. Bring to a boil and pour over chocolate. Working quickly, stir until chocolate is completely melted. Stir in liqueur and vanilla. Cool to room temperature in refrigerator. Beat with electric mixer until light and fluffy. Refrigerate bowl until cold and firm enough to handle, 1 to 2 hours. Form balls by hand and roll in cocoa, icing sugar and chopped nuts. Store in refrigerator.   **YIELD: 3 dozen**

SIMPLEST TRUFFLES *(see above)*

BURFI

· ·

A fudge-like East Indian sweet.

¾ cup	butter	175 mL
1 cup	white sugar	250 mL
1 cup	whole milk	250 mL
3½ cups	powdered milk	875 mL
1 cup	finely chopped almonds OR walnuts	250 mL
¼ cup	grated coconut	50 mL

In large heavy-bottomed saucepan, melt butter over low heat. Increase heat to medium-high and stir in sugar and milk. Bring to a boil and allow to boil for a few minutes, stirring often to avoid scorching. Decrease heat to low and gradually add powdered milk. Stir in nuts and coconut. Add more powdered milk if necessary to achieve the consistency of loose porridge. Remove from heat and beat with a spoon for a few minutes. Pour into buttered 8-in (20-cm) square pan. Keep refrigerated.   **YIELD: 64, 1-in (2.5-cm) squares**

· ·

PEANUT-BUTTERED POPCORN

This is an easy version of caramel corn.

½ cup	unpopped popcorn	125 mL
2 tbsp	vegetable oil	25 mL
½ cup	corn syrup	125 mL
½ cup	white sugar	125 mL
½ cup	peanut butter	125 mL
½ cup	salted peanuts	125 mL

In large saucepan or automatic popper, pop popcorn in oil. In medium saucepan, place corn syrup and sugar and bring to a boil. Remove from heat and stir in peanut butter and peanuts. Place popcorn in large bowl and pour on corn syrup mixture, stirring to distribute it evenly.   **YIELD: 3 qt (3 L)**

APRICOT NUT BALLS

These not-too-sweet candies are rolled in white sugar, giving them a pretty frosted effect.

2	eggs	2
1¼ cups	white sugar	300 mL
1 tsp	vanilla	5 mL
1 tsp	grated lemon rind	5 mL
1 cup	unsweetened coconut	250 mL
1 cup	chopped walnuts OR pecans	250 mL
½ cup	chopped dates	125 mL
½ cup	chopped apricots	125 mL

Preheat oven to 350°F (180°C). In large, ungreased casserole, beat eggs, ¾ cup (175 mL) sugar, vanilla and lemon rind. Stir in coconut, nuts, dates and apricots. Bake 30 minutes. Remove from oven. Stir until cool enough to handle. Shape into balls 1 in (2.5 cm) in diameter. Roll in remaining sugar.
YIELD: 2 dozen candies

CHOCOLATE-DIPPED PRETZELS

Although this may sound like a strange combination, the pretzel is just a medium for holding the chocolate in a pretty shape. They're very easy to dip and children really enjoy the novelty.

12 oz	white or dark semi-sweet chocolate	350 g
20-30	figure 8-shaped pretzels	20-30

In top of double boiler, melt chocolate. Remove from heat, leaving chocolate over hot water. With tongs, dip pretzels in melted chocolate, shaking off excess. Remove to wire cooling rack. Place waxed paper on surface under rack to catch dribbles. Allow to harden.   **YIELD: 20 to 30**

RUM BALLS OR BOURBON BALLS

This recipe can be found in just about every community cookbook published in North America, and with good reason. They are delicious and easy to make. You can substitute graham wafer crumbs for the vanilla cookies.

2 cups	fine vanilla cookie crumbs	500 mL
½ cup	cocoa	125 mL
1 cup	finely chopped pecans OR walnuts	250 mL
1 cup	icing sugar	250 mL
½ cup	melted butter	125 mL
½ cup	rum OR bourbon	125 mL
½ cup	icing sugar, white sugar, chocolate sprinkles, cocoa OR cookie crumbs	125 mL

In large bowl, combine crumbs, cocoa, nuts and icing sugar. Stir in melted butter and rum or bourbon. Shape into 1-in (2.5-cm) balls. Roll in sugar, chocolate sprinkles, cocoa or crumbs and place in sealed jar or tin in refrigerator. Allow to mellow 3 or 4 days before serving.   **YIELD: 3 dozen**

NO-COOK FOOD PROCESSOR FUDGE

. . . .

This super-easy, crystal-crunchy fudge requires no cooking.

8 oz	unsweetened chocolate squares	250 g
1 cup	butter	250 mL
1½ cups	sugar	375 mL
2 cups	finely chopped pecans OR walnuts	500 mL
¼ cup	heavy cream	50 mL

Grate chocolate in processor and remove to bowl. Replace grating blade with metal chopping blade. With a few on/off bursts, cream butter and 1 cup (250 mL) white sugar. Add grated chocolate and process to combine. Pat into bottom of 8-in (20-cm) square pan. Combine nuts, ½ cup (125 mL) sugar and cream in medium bowl and spread on chocolate base. Press to join 2 layers. Refrigerate. Cut when cold into 1-in (2.5-cm) squares.   **YIELD: 64 pieces**

. . . .

CANDIED PEEL

. . . .

The idea of making citrus peel edible must go back to the
time when an orange was a special once-a-year Christmas
treat and people couldn't bear to throw any of it out.
Homemade candied peel has the intense flavor of the zest
of oranges and especially lemons which we often use
in modern cooking. For a double whammy, dip the candied
peel in chocolate. Use lemon, orange, lime or grapefruit
peel, but cook them separately.

2 cups	citrus peel	500 mL
	Boiling water	
2½ cups	white sugar	625 mL
1 cup	water	250 mL

Cut peel into strips ⅓ in (82 mm) wide and place in medium
saucepan. Cover with boiling water and simmer for 5 minutes.
Boil more water. Drain peel and cover with boiling water.
Repeat this process 5 times. Meanwhile, place 2 cups (500 mL)
sugar and 1 cup (250 mL) water in medium saucepan over
medium heat. Stir until sugar is dissolved. Add cooked peel and
simmer at least 45 minutes until peel is soft and translucent.
Remove to wire rack on aluminum foil. Keep pieces separate.
When cool, sprinkle with remaining sugar and air dry for a
day.   **YIELD: 2 cups (500 mL)**

. . . .

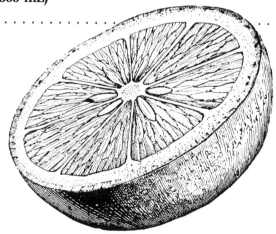

BREADS

There is an old saying about firewood, that it warms us twice: once when we chop it, and again when we burn it. I think that bread feeds us twice: once when we bake it and again when we eat it.

I am sorry to admit that I hardly ever bake bread. When I do, my family is all smiles. They practically get up and cheer when I make their favorite sticky buns. On the day I make them, the children hover around, watching the clock as the yeast bubbles and froths in a cup. They beg a little piece of dough as I knead together the flour and eggs, raisins and milk. They poke the puffed-out dough belly with their fingers and watch with fascination as I roll out the dough into an oblong and coat the surface with melted butter, cinnamon, brown sugar and pecans. While I roll it up, jelly-roll style, and cut it into a dozen even snails, they start to work up a feeding frenzy. Plates, glasses of milk and a chunk of cold butter are laid out on the table long before the bubbling brown buns are inverted on the cooling rack.

There is a wealth of Christmas bread recipes available to us. What they all have in common is that they take basic sweet dough and transform it into something special. Germans press slivered almonds and candied peel into the dough to make Stollen. Ukrainians ritually braid it into a circle and place a candle in the center. Russians roll it up with a mound of blue-black poppy seed and sprinkle on a light snow of icing sugar. Swedes color the dough with saffron and curl pieces into little kittens back to back.

I try to find the time to bake one of these breads for my family and to share with friends every year. Home baked bread is a treat, but Christmas bread is a double blessing.

BASIC SWEET BREAD DOUGH

½ cup	warm water	125 mL
2	packages dried yeast OR	2
2 tbsp	dried yeast	25 mL
1 cup	white sugar	250 mL
2 tsp	salt	10 mL
2-3	eggs	2-3
2 cups	milk at room temperature	500 mL
½ cup	melted butter	125 mL
7-8 cups	white flour, sifted and measured	1.75-2L
	Butter	

In a large bowl, place water and sprinkle on yeast and 1 tsp (5 mL) sugar. Stir and allow to soften until frothy, about 10 minutes. Beat in remaining sugar, salt, eggs, milk and melted butter. Stir in flour 1 cup (250 mL) at a time until too stiff to stir. *Note: If adding fruit or spices, do it at this point.* Knead in enough flour by hand to form a soft dough. Turn out onto lightly floured board and knead until smooth and shiny, about 5 minutes. Wash and butter bowl and place ball of dough in it. Butter top of dough. Cover with damp tea towel or plastic wrap. Place in warm spot until doubled in bulk, about 1 to 2 hours; dough that is heavy with fruit will take longer. Punch down and shape into loaves or rolls. Follow baking instructions for Braided Bread (page 134) or Poppy Seed Rolls (page 137).

An easy way to tell when dough is 'double in bulk' and ready for shaping: lightly press two fingertips about ½ in (2.5 cm) into risen dough. If an indentation remains, the dough is ready. When the dough has doubled in bulk, it should be punched down by pushing your fist quickly into the dough several times. Then pull the edges of the dough to the center and turn it over. It is now ready for shaping.

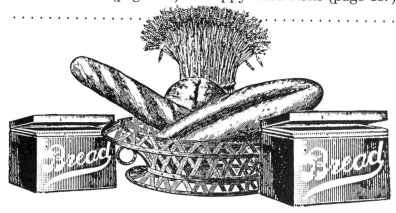

BRAIDED BREAD

You can use red and green cherries and nuts and colored sugar crystals in this bread.

1	recipe Basic Sweet Bread Dough (page 133)	1
1 cup	icing sugar	250 mL
1 tsp	lemon juice OR vanilla	5 mL
	Water	
1 cup	chopped candied peel and fruit	250 mL

Prepare Basic Sweet Bread recipe.

Preheat oven to 375°F (190°C). Divide dough into 3, 4, 5, or 6 even pieces. Roll pieces back and forth between palms of hands and lightly floured surface to form snakes, 1 in (2.5 cm) in diameter and 10 in (25 cm) long. Flour snakes and place side by side. At top end pinch together snakes to secure them. Number them in your head from left to right 1, 2, 3, 4, 5, 6. Pulling slightly, braid snake number one tightly over the next snake numbered in the list (e.g., in 3 plaits — 1 snake over 2 snake.) Then braid next snake over number listed (3 over 2). To repeat, go to top of list and repeat procedure (1 over 2), except for 6 plaits where first procedure is not repeated.

3 Plaits	4 Plaits	5 Plaits	6 Plaits
1 over 2	2 over 3	2 over 3	6 over 1 (do not repeat)
3 over 2	4 over 2	5 over 2	2 over 6
repeat	1 over 3	1 over	1 over 3
	repeat	repeat	5 over 1
			6 over 4
			2 over 6
			repeat

Finish ends by pinching together and folding them under. Place on buttered cookie sheets. Brush with melted butter. Allow to rise until double in bulk, about 30 minutes. Bake 30 to 40 minutes, until golden brown. Meanwhile, combine icing sugar and lemon juice or vanilla in small bowl. Stir in water, a few drops at a time, until it reaches the spreading consistency of white glue. Cover until ready to use. Remove breads from oven and, while still warm, spread on sugar glaze. Immediately sprinkle with bits of candied peel and glacéed fruit (red and green cherries), nuts, and/or colored sugar crystals.
YIELD: 3 large braided loaves

· ·

BRAIDED CHRISTMAS KALACH RING OR CHRISTMAS WREATH

In Russian and Ukrainian homes, this egg-rich bread is braided in a Christmas wreath, with a candle in the middle and placed on the table as a centerpiece.

Use Basic Sweet Bread Dough recipe using 1 more egg. After the dough has risen, punch it down and divide it into 3 even pieces. Roll it into long ropes. Braid ropes and join ends to form a circle. Place circle on buttered cookie sheet or for a more upright shape, in buttered tube pan. Cover and allow to rise until almost doubled. Brush with beaten egg diluted with 1 tbsp (15 mL) water. For baking, follow instructions for Braided Bread. For Christmas wreath, glaze and decorate with red and green cherries and colored sugar while still warm from the oven. **YIELD: 1 wreath**

POPPY SEED ROLLS

· ·

Prepare the filling and allow it to sit while you're mixing the dough.

4 cups	poppy seeds	1 L
	Boiling water	
1 cup	chopped raisins	250 mL
2 cups	chopped walnuts	500 mL
½ cup	honey	125 mL
1 tsp	grated lemon rind	5 mL
1	egg white	1
1	recipe Basic Sweet Bread Dough (page 133)	1

Glaze

1	egg	1
1 tbsp	water	15 mL

In large bowl, place poppy seed. Cover with boiling water and allow to cool. Drain well through sieve. Grind poppy seed a few times through a hand grinder or process briefly in food processor. Add raisins, walnuts, honey, lemon rind and egg white. Prepare Basic Sweet Bread recipe. Preheat oven to 375°F (190°C). Pull apart dough into 4 pieces. Place all but 1 piece back in bowl and cover. Roll out other piece on lightly floured surface to form an oval 12 × 9 in (30 × 22.5 cm) and ¼ in (6 mm) thick. Spread poppy seed filling evenly over dough surface leaving 1 in (2.5 cm) around all edges. Starting with one long side, roll the dough up to form a flat jelly roll. Pinch ends to seal. Place seam side down on buttered cookie sheets. Allow to rise until almost double in bulk, about 45 minutes. In a cup, beat together egg and water to make glaze and brush on rolls. Bake 25 to 30 minutes until golden brown. Do not crowd in oven.
YIELD: 4 rolls

· ·

STICKY CINNAMON BUNS

Follow instructions for Basic Sweet Bread Dough.

1	recipe Basic Sweet Bread Dough (page 133)	1
1 cup	raisins	250 mL
1 cup & 3 tbsp	melted butter, divided	300 mL
3 tbsp	cinnamon	50 mL
2¼ cups	brown sugar, divided	550 mL
1 cup	finely chopped walnuts OR pecans	250 mL
1½ cups	corn syrup	375 mL

Preheat oven to 350°F (180°C). Follow instructions for Basic Sweet Bread Dough recipe, adding raisins while kneading flour. Divide dough into 3 equal balls. Place 3 balls back in bowl and cover. Roll out 1 ball to form a 10 × 18-in (25 × 45-cm) rectangle. Sprinkle ⅓ cup (75 mL) melted butter, then 1 tbsp (15 mL) cinnamon, ½ cup (125 mL) brown sugar, ⅓ cup (75 mL) walnuts or pecans over dough evenly to edges. Starting at 1 long edge, roll up tightly, to form a cylinder. Pinch edges and ends to seal. Cut cylinder into cross-sections about 2 in (5 cm) thick. Generously butter bottom and sides of three 8-in (20-cm) square or round baking pans. Spread ½ cup (125 mL) corn syrup evenly on bottom of each pan. Sprinkle ¼ cup (50 mL) brown sugar on each pan. Place 1 roll of buns, swirl side up, touching, in each pan. Repeat procedure with other balls of dough. Brush buns with 3 tbsp (50 mL) melted butter. Allow to rise until double in bulk, about 45 minutes. Bake 30 to 35 minutes until golden. Do not crowd in oven. Cook in separate batches if necessary to avoid uneven browning. Place cookie sheet on rack below buns, as syrup sometimes bubbles over. Make sure bun in center of pan is cooked through before removing pan from oven. Remove from oven, loosen edges with knife and immediately invert on cooling rack; otherwise, buns will stick to pan. Be careful not to burn yourself with hot corn syrup. Place waxed paper on counter under rack to ease cleanup.

YIELD: 2 to 2½ dozen buns.

. . . .

SWEDISH SAFFRON BUNS (SAFFRONSBROD)

These buns are traditionally served with steaming coffee as a breakfast-in-bed treat on St. Lucia's Day (December 13) in Scandinavia. This day marks the beginning of the Christmas holidays. The buns are served by the eldest daughter of the household dressed up as St. Lucia (a beautiful Christian martyr) in long flowing robes and a whortleberry crown with lighted candles.

⅓ tsp	saffron threads	1.5 mL
2 tbsp	boiling water	25 mL
1	recipe Basic Sweet Bread Dough (page 133)	1
2 tsp	grated orange rind	10 mL
1	egg	1
1 tsp	water	5 mL
½ cup	raisins	125 mL

In a small bowl, place saffron and boiling water. Set aside to cool. Prepare Basic Sweet Bread Dough recipe, adding orange rind when kneading flour. Preheat oven to 400°F (200°C). Punch down dough and divide it into 54 pieces. To shape the buns to curl up like Lucia's cats, back to back: roll each piece into a sausage shape ¾ in (19 mm) thick and 6 in (15 cm) long. Take 2 strands of dough and place them touching side by side. Join them by pinching centers together. Take 2 top ends and form curlicues away from each other and down towards the center. Take 2 bottom ends and form curlicues away from each other and up towards the center. Place on buttered cookie sheets a few inches apart. Poke raisins in center of curlicues. Cover and let rise until double, about 30 minutes. Beat together egg and water in small cup. Brush egg glaze on buns. Bake 15 to 20 minutes until golden brown.   **YIELD: 27 buns**

STUFFED TURKEY BREAST *(see page 159)*
with APPLE PRUNE STUFFING *(see page 160)*

CHAPTER 5

CHRISTMAS DINNERS

THE CELEBRATION FEAST

*T*his is it! Christmas is here. The realization comes in different ways: in a still moment at church Christmas Eve during the singing of "O Holy Night" or in a sigh after the last present has been wrapped and snuck under the tree. Preparation time is over. What has not been done will not be done. It is time to feast and have a good time. 🐟 Our ancestors celebrated at this time of year thousands of years before the birth of Christ. Maybe that is why no matter what our religious commitment, it is a holiday that captures our imagination. 🐟 Around the world, people feast on both Christmas Eve and Christmas Day. While North Americans usually have their big meal on Christmas Day, it may be at noon or eight o'clock at night. I serve dinner around five o'clock to give me a relaxing morning for preparation and a meal that is not too late for the children to enjoy. Friends with two sets of grandparents are expected to eat two full dinners that day and head out to the first one at noon. 🐟 Eastern Europeans, Germans and Scandinavians start feasting on Christmas Eve. Ukrainians and Poles who follow tradition enjoy a 12-course meatless meal symbolic of the 12 apostles. Because Advent, beginning four Sundays before Christmas, was a time of penance in the Catholic Church, red meat was traditionally forbidden and the pre-midnight meals were meatless. Italians also eat a fish meal on Christmas Eve. Because of the midnight mass service, Catholics have food traditions tied to the time before and after church attendance. French-Canadians have their wake-up party, réveillon, after mass and serve their famous pork pie, tourtière. A friend of mine who grew up in Paris remembers the thrill of coming home from mass at 1 a.m. to fresh baked brioche and hot chocolate. Food traditions linger even after the religious reasons are gone. One friend of mine, a third-generation Canadian of Polish descent who no longer attends church, still celebrates the evening of December 24 with an elegant seafood dinner. ▨ By setting aside a day for feasting and sharing ritual foods with our neighbors, we renew our bonds to our community. When we prepare dishes handed down to us from our grandmothers, we become grandchildren again, reconnected to the people who have gone before us. When we prepare traditional foods for our children, we give them memories they can turn to when they are grown and cut adrift. They will prepare these foods and once again be grounded with their families in time. ▨ We are lucky to live in a time of choice. Although *lutfisk*, a sundried, lime-soaked ling cod is a traditional Swedish Christmas dish, modern Swedes have the option to serve fresh fish instead. We don't have to be French-Canadian to enjoy tourtière, or English to flambé a plum pudding. ▨ We create our own traditions by doing the same things over and over again, because they give us joy. I know a family who has given up plum pudding for chocolate mousse. They look forward to spending a part of Christmas day in the kitchen, whipping it up together. I wish that there was some way that I could, by following their recipe, re-create the special magic that it has come to mean to them. ▨ Christmas comes at the end of our annual cycle. December 21 or 22 is the shortest day of the year, and after that we look forward to more daylight and sunshine with renewed hope for the new year. Whether we assign it a religious connotation with the birth of the Christ Child or prefer the more basic, pagan reasons, Christmas is a profound celebration that touches most of us.

Pulling together the big dinner

Christmas morning, and here I sit cross-legged on the floor. While the children tear open presents, I tear apart bread for stuffing. Later, when they are having a fine time outside playing in the snow, I will still be in the kitchen.

For the cook, Christmas is work. There is no getting around it. To set the record straight, I don't mind the work, even the pressure. I love pulling together Christmas dinner. But it is a job. Christmas dinner is work because your average meatloaf-for-three cook is suddenly expected to prepare a five-course meal for a dozen people. The cook's challenge is to prepare a complex meal while maintaining the strength and good humor to enjoy it.

I look forward to Boxing Day. On Boxing Day I wake up in a state of delicious calm because I know that today is the day I do not cook. We eat wonderful leftovers or get fed by someone else.

Planning the menu

The temptation is to go all out, but in order to avoid Christmas dinner burnout, the most important thing is to keep the menu reasonable. I start with a list of all the things I would *like* to serve, a tempting list of possibilities. Then I go through it and mark all the dishes that are essential to everyone's enjoyment and sense of tradition. The final menu gets honed down by taking the following things into consideration:

◆ the number of people and the amount of food to prepare
◆ individual tastes and preferences
◆ the time it takes to prepare the food
◆ the energy level of the cook
◆ aesthetics: I think in three-D color: beige turkey, white potatoes, green peas. Add some purple beets, orange squash and red cabbage.

Getting it on the table, piping hot

Because freshness is my highest priority, I leave most of the food preparation to Christmas Day. That's my choice, because I don't like warmed up anything. The two hours before the first bite, therefore, are extremely hectic in my kitchen. I usually enlist some help. The strongest arm mashes potatoes. The most skillful swordsman slices the turkey. Little hands deliver pats of butter and bowls of sauce to the table. Others fill glasses.

Every cook has his or her own system. At the opposite end of the spectrum from me is an acquaintance who roasts and slices her turkey and freezes it along with the gravy weeks before Christmas. She simply reheats the food and pops it on the table. For her, being with her company is more important.

We all make freshness compromises. Rolls baked a week before Christmas, frozen and reheated are much better than storebought, or no rolls at all. Some cooks prepare their vegetables early in the morning and leave them soaking in cold water until cooking time. There may be a minor loss of vitamins, but a gain in peace of mind, which in the long run may be much healthier for everyone.

For years, Christmas vegetables were kept warm in ovens and over hot water in double boilers. The invention of the microwave oven is a boon because it does such a good job of reheating food. I mash the potatoes, place them in a serving dish and cover them with plastic wrap. I wash the cooking pot and put it away well before the china from the meal has to be washed. A few minutes before the turkey is sliced I start cooking and reheating vegetables. The only problem is juggling the various dishes that are waiting to be popped in and out of the microwave.

I usually carve the turkey in the kitchen, but I have a friend who loves the aesthetics of bringing the big bird to the dining room table. She says that after all the time in the kitchen she likes to set aside a few moments to relish the beauty of the meal.

Cleanup

Because I am not one myself, I have always admired quiet methodical cooks who clean up their messes as they go along. There are four stages to cleanup:

1 mixing bowls, utensils, food machines, pots and pans from food preparation
2 pots and pans used as holding containers for food and keeping things hot, making gravy, etc.
3 serving platters and bowls, china, silverware and glasses
4 coffee and tea cups, dessert dishes

Cleanup is easier if attacked at different stages. Try to get the food preparation dishes out of the way before the meal. Put the dinner plates in to soak or in the dishwasher before serving dessert.

After the meal it is the cook's turn to sit it out. Get someone else to do the dishes. The performance is over.

At the very least, don't relinquish this time to savor your accomplishment by rushing back into the kitchen to do the dishes. They will still be there tomorrow.

. . . .

PERFECT TURKEY

From the moment my eyes reluctantly pop open Christmas morning, throughout the squeals of delight during present opening, I must confess that there is only one thing on my mind: getting the turkey stuffed, sewn up and in the oven. It's simple: no turkey, no Christmas. And everyone is depending on me.

Buying the turkey

Most turkeys sold today are small (under 12 lb/5.44 kg). For every ¾-1 lb (350-500 g) expect one serving.

If you are cooking a larger turkey for a crowd, allow ½-¾ lb (250-375 g) per serving.

Number of Servings	Weight in Pounds	Weight in Kg
6-10	6-8	2.7-3.6
10-20	8-12	3.6-5.4
20-32	12-16	5.4-7.2
32-40	16-20	7.2-9

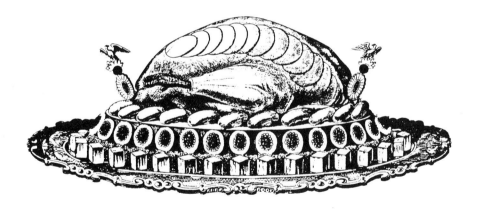

Defrosting the turkey

Once the turkey is thawed, roast it immediately or place it in the refrigerator.

IN THE REFRIGERATOR
Leave bird in original wrapping. It will take about 5 hours/lb or 2¼ hours/kg of turkey (24 hours for 5 lb; 48 hours for 10 lb) to thaw.

IN COLD WATER
Leave bird in original wrapping. It will take about 1 hour/lb or 27 minutes/kg of turkey (5 hours for 5 lb; 10 hours for 10 lb) to thaw.

AT ROOM TEMPERATURE
Leave bird in original wrapping. It will take about 1½ hours/lb or 40 minutes/kg (7½ hours for 5 lb of turkey; 15 hours for 10 lb) to thaw.

IN A MICROWAVE OVEN
Follow manufacturer's instructions.

Getting the turkey ready for the oven

Preheat the oven to 325°F (160°C). Remove the giblets (neck, heart, liver, gizzard). Place them in a small saucepan with 1 whole onion and enough water to cover. Bring to a boil; cover and simmer 2 or 3 hours. This makes a wonderful broth for gravy later.

Place the turkey in the sink and let cold water run through the cavity. Drain it well and pat it dry. To avoid contaminating other foods with raw turkey microbes, wash your hands, knives, counters, etc. with hot soapy water often.

Place the turkey in a roasting pan and stuff it.

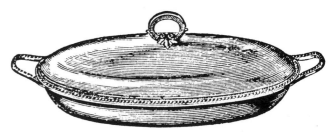

Stuffing the turkey

Stuffing measurements are very approximate considering the variables, such as the shape of the bird and the moisture content and density of the stuffing.

Allow approximately ½ to ¾ cup (125 to 175 mL) of stuffing for each pound (500 g) of turkey. Fill the cavity only three-quarters full to leave room for swelling.

Weight in Pounds/Kg	Cups of Stuffing	Litres of Stuffing
6-8 lb (2.7-3.6 kg)	4-5	1-1.25
8-12 lb (3.6-5.4 kg)	7-8	1.75-2
12-16 lb (5.4-7.2 kg)	10-11	2.5-2.75
16-20 lb (7.2-9 kg)	13-14	3.25-3.5

If using stuffing prepared the day before, place it, cold, from the refrigerator into the cold bird.

Place turkey, breast side down. If neck skin is intact, place 1-2 cups (250-500 mL) stuffing in skin flap. Pull skin to back and secure with skewer or by sewing shut with needle and thread.

Prop turkey with legs and cavity upright. Fill body cavity three-quarters full. Close cavity with skewer or by sewing with needle and thread.

Trussing the turkey

Place turkey in roasting pan breast side up.

Cut an 8 to 10 ft (2.5 to 3 m) piece of strong cotton string or butcher's twine.

Cross legs and tie a double knot to hold them together.

With a string in both hands, bring strings under bird in a criss-cross pattern. Bring strings up on each side of turkey, pulling up wings. Bring strings to top of breast and tie securely. Leave trussed turkey in the roasting pan breast side up.

Rub the skin with melted butter or vegetable oil. Sometimes I sprinkle on a dusting of white flour or bread crumbs which brown and keep the skin soft and delicious.

Roasting the stuffed turkey

Cook turkey at 325°F (160°C). I had never been able to figure out why the cooking times for turkey varied so much from book to book until I came across this sound advice in the 1945 edition of the *Purity Cook Book*, a publication of Purity Flour Mills, Toronto: "There can be no set rules for roasting poultry. The size, weight and shape of the bird and personal taste will each have an influence. The times given in a table are therefore only approximate."

Marie Nightingale, a food writer from Nova Scotia, says that the younger turkeys available today do not take as long to cook as the larger older birds used to. She recommends never roasting it at a temperature higher than 325°F (160°C) to avoid overcooking.

So here is the best approximate advice I can give for roasting a stuffed turkey at 325°F (160°C):

Small turkey (under 10 lb) . . . . about 20 min/lb
Medium turkey (10-15 lb) . . . . about 15 min/lb
Large turkey (over 15 lb) . . . . about 12 min/lb
Small turkey (under 4.5 kg) . . . . about 44 min/kg
Medium turkey (4.5-6.8 kg) . . . . about 33 min/kg
Large turkey (over 6.8 kg) . . . . about 26 min/kg

Note: pre-basted turkeys may take up to 20 per cent less time to cook than basted birds. Follow the instructions on package.

During the last hour, while basting, check the thermometer and for other signs of doneness.

The turkey is cooked when:
♦ a meat thermometer in the thigh meat registers 180° to 185°F (82° to 85°C)
♦ the stuffing should reach a temperature of 165°F (75°C)
♦ the drumstick twists easily
♦ the juices run clear
♦ the leg joints are not pink

Carving the turkey

Remove the turkey from the oven and allow it to sit at room temperature for 20 minutes, on a clean cutting board or platter.

Meanwhile, make the gravy with the pan juices in the roasting pan.

TOOLS

1 very sharp long knife
1 large fork
1 or more platters on which to place sliced meat
1 large spoon for scooping out stuffing
1 bowl in which to place stuffing

Carving is an art as much as it is a science. Here are a few guidelines but experience is the best teacher. I encourage anyone who is willing, to carve the turkey because I am usually very busy with other details of the meal.

With the fork in one hand and the knife in the other, steady the turkey by piercing the top of the bird with the fork.

On one side of the turkey:

1 Cut the leg and thigh together by slicing between the breast and thigh. Locate the hip joint and slice through it.
2 Find the joint between the leg and the thigh and cut through it.
3 Cut the thigh into several pieces.
4 Cut down through the breast to the wing. Find the socket joint and sever it, releasing the wing.
5 Steady the fork into one side of the breast and slice diagonally down through to remove slices of breast meat.
6 Now repeat the above instructions on the other side of the turkey.

ALMOST-NEVER-FAIL GRAVY

Friends complain to me that their gravy always flops, so I am including my method. It has never failed for me, but I shudder to put a foolproof label on any recipe.

	Turkey giblets (heart, gizzard, liver, neck)	
1	onion	1
¼ cup	white flour	50 mL
	Jar with screw-top lid	
	Wire whisk	
	Salt and freshly ground pepper to taste	

After putting turkey in oven, place turkey giblets and whole peeled onion in medium saucepan. Add cold water to cover. Over high heat, bring to a boil. Reduce heat, cover and simmer 2 to 3 hours. Remove from heat. Measure broth and add water if necessary to make up 2 cups (500 mL). Set aside. When turkey is cooked and set on platter or cutting board, place flour and 1 cup (250 mL) cooled turkey broth in jar with a lid. Cover and shake jar to dissolve flour. Place metal or enamel roaster on low heat. Add remaining clear turkey broth, stirring up bits on bottom. Stir in flour/broth mixture and increase heat to medium. Continue stirring with whisk until thickened. If paste forms, thin with more turkey broth or water to desired consistency. Add salt and freshly ground pepper to taste. Remove to gravy boat, or if not serving immediately, to saucepan or small microwave safe bowl for reheating.   **YIELD: about 2 cups (500 mL)**

MUSHROOM GRAVY

2 cups	sliced fresh mushrooms	500 mL
2-4 tbsp	butter	25-60 mL

Use standard gravy recipe. Sauté mushrooms in butter until wilted with crisp edges and add to gravy at end of recipe.

STUFFINGS FOR TURKEY, GOOSE, CHICKEN AND DUCK

Allow ½ cup (125 mL) stuffing per pound (500 g) of bird. Fill the cavity only three-quarters full to leave room for expansion.

PLAIN OLD-FASHIONED POTATO STUFFING

What could be simpler? And you don't have to serve mashed potatoes on the side.

4 cups	**hot mashed potatoes**	**1 L**
¼ cup	**butter, bacon fat OR vegetable oil**	**50 mL**
1	**onion**	**1**
1 cup	**sliced fresh mushrooms (optional)**	**250 mL**
½ tsp	**sage**	**2 mL**
½ tsp	**summer savory**	**2 mL**
	Salt and freshly ground pepper to taste	

Prepare potatoes and set aside. In large skillet, warm butter, bacon fat or oil. Add onion and sauté until transparent. If using mushrooms, add and sauté until slightly crisp and brown. Add potatoes, sage, savory, salt and freshly ground pepper to taste.   **YIELD: 4 to 5 cups (1 to 1.25 L), enough for a 7 to 10 lb (3 to 4.5 kg) bird**

To keep the leftovers: Remove all stuffing from the turkey before refrigeration to avoid contamination in the cavity of the bird.

Refrigerate cooked meat within 2 hours of removing from the oven. Wrap it well and use it within 2 to 3 days. Or seal and freeze it but use it within a month.

DRIED FRUIT, NUT AND RICE STUFFING

. . . .

Use cashews, almonds, pistachios, pine nuts.

2 cups	white rice	500 mL
4 cups	water OR chicken broth	1 L
¼ cup	butter	50 mL
1	small onion	1
½ cup	nuts	125 mL
1 cup	chopped dried fruit	250 mL
	Salt and freshly ground pepper	

In large saucepan, place rice and water or broth over high heat. Bring to a boil, cover and reduce heat to simmer until rice is soft, about 20 minutes. Meanwhile, in medium saucepan, melt butter. Finely dice onion and sauté with nuts until onion is soft. Add all ingredients to rice.   **YIELD: 4 to 5 cups (1 to 1.25 mL), enough for a 7 to 10 lb (3 to 4.5 kg) bird**

. . . .

ITALIAN RICE STUFFING

. . . .

This is reminiscent of the stuffing Thomasine Boni remembers her mother making in the 1920s.

2 cups	white rice	500 mL
4 cups	water OR chicken broth	1 L
¼ cup	melted butter	50 mL
2	eggs	2
2-4 tbsp	Parmesan cheese	25-60 mL
¼ cup	fresh parsley	50 mL
½ tsp	grated whole nutmeg	2 mL
	Salt and freshly ground pepper	

Place rice and water or broth in large saucepan over high heat. Bring to a boil, cover and reduce heat to simmer until rice is soft, about 20 minutes. Remove from heat and cool before adding remaining ingredients.   **YIELD: 4 to 5 cups (1 to 1.25 mL), enough for a 7 to 10 lb (3 to 4.5 kg) bird**

. . . .

MY FAVORITE BREAD AND WILD MUSHROOM STUFFING

I use mushrooms which I have picked in the fall, fried in butter and frozen. You can use rendered turkey or chicken fat instead of butter.

4-6 tbsp	butter	60-90 mL
1	onion	1
1	rib celery	1
2 cups	sliced fresh or frozen mushrooms	500 mL
1	medium potato	1
1	small carrot	1
4-6 cups	cubed fresh bread	1-1.5 L
2 tbsp	frozen peas	25 mL
1 tbsp	fresh sage OR	15 mL
1 tsp	dried sage	5 mL
1 tbsp	fresh summer savory OR	15 mL
1 tsp	dried summer savory	5 mL
2 tbsp	fresh parsley	25 mL
	Salt and freshly ground pepper to taste	

In large skillet, melt butter. Finely chop onion and celery and add to skillet. Sauté until transparent. Increase heat to medium-high. Add sliced mushrooms and fry for 5 minutes, stirring often, until mushrooms are reduced in volume and slightly crisp. Peel and grate potato and carrot. Add to mushroom mixture. Stir for a few minutes over medium heat. Place bread cubes in large bowl. Stir in mushroom mixture, peas, sage, summer savory, salt and freshly ground pepper to taste.   **YIELD: 4 to 5 cups (1 to 1.25 mL), enough for a 7 to 10 lb (3 to 4.5 kg) bird**

SAUSAGE STUFFING

¾ lb	raw sausage meat	375 g
4 cups	fresh fine bread crumbs	1 L
¼ cup	minced celery	50 mL
¼ tsp	grated lemon rind	1 mL
½ tsp	sage OR thyme	2 mL
	Salt and freshly ground pepper	

Remove sausage meat from casing. Crumble and place in large skillet over medium-high heat. Fry until no longer pink in color, stirring and mashing to break down chunks. In a large bowl, place bread crumbs, and pour contents of skillet over top. Add celery and grated lemon rind. Depending on flavor of sausage, adjust seasoning to your taste. Mix well.   **YIELD: 4 to 5 cups (1-1.25 L), enough for a 7 to 10 lb (3 to 4.5 kg) bird**

OYSTER STUFFING

¼ cup	butter	50 mL
1	onion	1
1	rib celery	1
½	carrot	½
3 cups	cubed fresh bread	750 mL
½ tsp	sage	2 mL
½ tsp	summer savory	2 mL
2 tbsp	fresh parsley	25 mL
1 tsp	grated lemon rind	5 mL
	Salt and freshly ground pepper	
1-2 cups	cooked or canned oysters, drained	250-500 mL

In large skillet, melt butter over medium-low heat. Mince onion, celery and carrot. Add to skillet and sauté until onion is transparent. In large bowl, toss bread cubes with sage, summer savory, parsley, lemon rind, salt and pepper to taste. Stir in onion mixture and oysters.   **YIELD: 4 to 5 cups (1 to 1.25 mL) enough for a 7 to 10 lb (3 to 4.5 kg) bird**

CRANBERRY SAUCES

Cranberry sauce is a Christmas classic made simply with two parts cranberries, to one part sugar and one part water.

Sugar and water are boiled to produce a medium syrup. Fresh cranberries are added and simmered gently. Set aside to cool, the mixture gels into sauce because the cranberries are full of pectin. You can vary the taste by adding a few spices (cloves, cinnamon stick or allspice berries) or dried fruit (raisins, currants, chopped apricots) while cooking. Stir in some grated orange or lemon peel at the end, or cook with fruit juice instead of water.

Make it a week before or the same day you want to eat it. But allow a few hours for it to cool and gel. If you like a warm, liquid sauce, make it at the last minute.

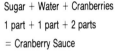

Sugar + Water + Cranberries
1 part + 1 part + 2 parts
= Cranberry Sauce

TRADITIONAL STOVE TOP CRANBERRY SAUCE

2 cups	white sugar	500 mL
2 cups	water	500 mL
4 cups	whole fresh cranberries	1 L

In large saucepan, place sugar and water over high heat. Boil 5 minutes. Reduce heat to low and stir in cranberries. Simmer, uncovered, without stirring for 5 minutes. Pour into serving dish or mold. Set aside to cool. Cover and refrigerate until serving.   **YIELD: 3½ cups (875 mL)**

FRESH CRANBERRY SAUCE

This uncooked sauce also makes a juicy refreshing dessert with an almost tropical flavor.

1	apple	1
1	orange	1
2 cups	fresh whole cranberries	500 mL
¼ cup	blanched almonds	50 mL
½ cup	white sugar	125 mL

Wash and scrub apple and orange but do not peel. Quarter and remove seeds. Coarsely chop cranberries, almonds and prepared apple and orange in food processor. Place in glass or ceramic bowl or jar. Stir in sugar and refrigerate 1 day before serving.   **YIELD: 2 to 2½ cups (500 to 625 mL)**

MICROWAVE CRANAPPLE SAUCE

2	apples	2
1 cup	fresh whole cranberries	250 mL
½ cup	water	125 mL
¼ cup	currants	50 mL
1-2 tbsp	white sugar	15-25 mL

Peel, core and chop apples. In 4-cup (1-L) microwave safe glass bowl place all ingredients, and cover with plastic wrap. Cook on High 4 to 5 minutes, stirring halfway through. Stir until smooth. Serve hot or cold.   **YIELD: 1½ cups (375 mL)**

SMALL FEASTS

· ·

TINY TURKEY OR
STUFFED TURKEY BREAST

· ·

Here is a feast for a single person or small family who likes turkey but not the leftovers. Two turkey breasts are sewn together to make a 4-lb (2-kg) turkey which then can be stuffed. Use breasts with bone and skin still attached.

2	turkey breast halves, about 2 lb (1 kg) each	2
2 tbsp	soft butter	25 mL
2 cups	Apple-Prune Stuffing (recipe follows)	500 mL

Preheat over to 350°F (180°C). With knife, carefully remove large bones, leaving smaller ones. Place 1 breast half, skin side down, on flat surface. Place stuffing on breast. Top with other breast, skin side up. Sew 2 pieces together, stretching skin and stitching around edges. Place in small roaster. Rub with butter so breast meat won't dry out. Loosely cover with foil and roast 1 hour. Baste often during cooking. Remove foil and allow to brown, continuing to cook for about 1 hour. Make gravy with pan juices if you like. Remove thread, carve and serve.
YIELD: 2 to 4 servings

· ·

APPLE-PRUNE STUFFING FOR TINY TURKEY

1 cup	fine fresh bread crumbs	250 mL
1 tbsp	melted butter	15 mL
½	apple, finely diced	½
4	pitted prunes, chopped	4
1 tsp	finely grated onion	5 mL
	Salt and freshly ground pepper to taste	

In medium bowl, place bread crumbs and stir in butter. Add diced apple, chopped prunes, onion, salt and pepper. Mix well.   **YIELD: 1 cup (250 mL)**

ROCK CORNISH GAME HEN WITH WILD RICE STUFFING

A rock Cornish game hen is a small, 1 to 2 lb (500 g to 1 kg) chicken. Roasted and stuffed, it can be just as festive as a turkey 10 times its size, and is a reasonable serving for one or two people. Fill it with ½ cup (125 mL) of your favorite stuffing or Wild Rice Stuffing. For three to five people, roast three birds, triple the stuffing recipe and increase the cooking time accordingly.

1	rock Cornish game hen	1
½ cup	Wild Rice Stuffing (recipe follows)	125 mL
1 tbsp each	butter AND white flour OR	15 mL each
1 tbsp	marmalade	15 mL

Preheat oven to 400°F (200°C). Rinse bird and pat dry. Fill cavity with stuffing and skewer or sew vent closed with thread. Rub hen with butter and dust with flour or rub with marmalade. Roast uncovered for about 45 minutes until hen reaches an internal temperature of 180°F (80°C). Baste frequently with pan juices.   **YIELD: 1 to 2 servings**

WILD RICE STUFFING

You can use pine nuts, cashews or pecans.

2 cups	water	500 mL
¼ cup	wild rice	50 mL
	Pinch salt	
2 tsp	butter	10 mL
1 tbsp	finely diced onion	15 mL
1 tbsp	finely chopped nuts	15 mL
1 tsp	dried currants	5 mL
	Salt and freshly ground pepper to taste	

Wash and rinse rice several times to remove floating particles. In a saucepan, bring water to a rolling boil. Add wild rice and salt. Reduce heat, cover, and simmer for 40 minutes, until rice particles split open and curl back. Drain well. Meanwhile, in a skillet, melt butter and sauté onion, nuts and currants 2 to 3 minutes until onion is translucent. Combine rice, onion mixture and salt and pepper to taste in skillet. Remove from heat and cool to room temperature before handling.

YIELD: ½ cup (125 mL), enough for 1 bird

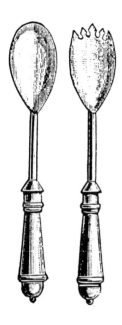

OTHER TRADITIONAL DISHES

. . . .

ROAST GOOSE WITH PRUNES AND APPLES

. . . .

For a Scandinavian-style goose dinner, serve with applesauce, lingonberry or cranberry sauce, braised red cabbage, sugar-browned potatoes, gingerbread cookies, glogg and Danish rice porridge.

For a British-style goose dinner, substitute a bread sage stuffing for the prunes and apples and serve it with bread sauce, brussels sprouts, turnip or parsnips, peas, oven-roasted potatoes, red currant jelly, eggnog, mince pies and plum pudding.

24	large pitted prunes	24
1½ cups	apple juice	375 mL
4-6	apples	4-6
1	onion	1
8-10 lb	goose	4-5 kg
½	fresh lemon	½
	Salt and freshly ground pepper to taste	

Preheat oven to 325°F (160°C). In medium bowl, combine prunes and apple juice. Set aside for 1 hour. Drain prunes and return to bowl. Peel, quarter and core apples. Add apple, chopped onion, salt and freshly ground pepper to taste, to bowl. Toss to combine. Rinse goose under running cold water. Drain and pat dry. Pull out all fat inside the body cavity. Rub lemon inside and outside goose. Stuff with prune mixture. Sew or skewer cavity closed. Place goose on rack in roasting pan. Prick skin all over to release fat during roasting. Do not baste. Bake about 2 to 2½ hours (20 to 25 min/lb and 50 to 45 min/kg) until an internal temperature of 185°F (85°C) is reached. During roasting, remove accumulating fat from pan every 30 minutes or so.   **YIELD: 4 to 6 servings**

. . . .

BREAD SAUCE

· ·

1	medium onion	1
3-6	whole cloves	3-6
1	bay leaf	1
2 cups	milk	500 mL
3 cups	fine soft bread crumbs	750 mL
¼ cup	butter	50 mL
	Salt and freshly ground pepper to taste	
1-2 tbsp	cream	15-25 mL

In a large saucepan, heat onion, bay leaf, milk, salt and pepper over medium heat. Stir occasionally until mixture comes almost to a boil. Remove from heat and allow to steep 20 minutes. Remove onion and bay leaf and discard. Place back on low heat and gradually stir in bread crumbs, to form a thick smooth sauce. Add salt and freshly ground pepper to taste and thin with cream to desired consistency.
YIELD: 2 cups (500 mL)

· ·

CHRISTMAS EVE VEGETARIAN BORSCHT

· ·

This clear meatless beet soup is a traditional Christmas Eve dish in Polish and Ukrainian homes. A few generations ago, a root cellar full of beets, potatoes and other root crops was common. Wild mushrooms were picked and dried by many rural people of Eastern European extraction. Today, fresh beets are hard to find in the stores at Christmastime and, dried boletuses have become an expensive gourmet item. We offer a substitution of less intensely flavored cultivated fresh mushrooms. What used to be poor man's food (cheap like borscht) just isn't so anymore.

½ cup	dried boletuses (cepe, steinpiltz) mushrooms OR	125 mL
1 cup	diced fresh mushrooms	250 mL
	Boiling water	
2 tbsp	vegetable oil	25 mL
1	onion	1
1	clove garlic	1
1	stalk celery	1
1	carrot	1
4	fresh beets	4
3 cups	coarsely chopped cabbage	750 mL
28 oz	canned tomatoes including liquid	800 mL
	Fresh parsley	
	Salt and freshly ground pepper to taste	
¼-½ cup	brown sugar	50-125 mL
¼-½ cup	lemon juice, wine vinegar OR herb vinegar	50-125 mL

In small saucepan, place mushrooms and cover with boiling water. Simmer 30 minutes. Peel and coarsely chop onion, garlic, celery and carrot. Peel and grate fresh beets. In Dutch oven or large heavy-bottomed stock pot, warm oil and sauté onion, garlic, celery and carrot. Add beets, cabbage, mushrooms and mushroom water, canned tomatoes and parsley. Add water to cover, about 6 cups (1.5 L). Bring to a boil, reduce heat, cover and simmer 1 to 2 hours. Remove from heat. Cool slightly and pour over colander into large bowl, straining out all solids. Discard solids or use in other recipe. Add salt and pepper to soup. To achieve sweet and sour balance, stir in brown sugar and lemon juice or vinegar 1 tbsp (15 mL) at a time, tasting after each addition.   **YIELD: 2 qt (2 L)**

. . . .

CHRISTMAS EVE VEGETARIAN BORSCHT
(see above)

SPAGHETTINI WITH ANCHOVY SAUCE

Christmas Eve was special to Fran Boni Whitelaw because her father, Frank, prepared supper. His specialty was this meatless Italian dish.

3	whole salted anchovies	80 g
	OR	
1 oz	canned anchovies	30 g
2-3	garlic cloves	2-3
⅓ cup	quality olive oil	75 mL
½ cup	black Greek olives	125 mL
¼ cup	snipped fresh parsley	50 mL
¾ lb	spaghettini	375 g

For whole salted anchovies, soak in water 30 minutes. Drain, skin, bone and fillet. Pat dry and chop very fine. For canned anchovies, drain off oil, and rinse with warm water. Drain, pat dry and chop very fine. In small saucepan, warm oil. Mince garlic and sauté for 1 minute. Stir in anchovies to form a paste. Pit and chop olives and add to saucepan along with parsley. Serve immediately over freshly boiled spaghettini.

YIELD: 3 to 4 servings.

GISELE GAUVIN'S TOURTIÈRE

Tourtière is derived from the French words for "pigeon pie." The term is believed to have originated in the 16th century when wild pigeons were abundant in New France and consequently put into pies.

Jackie Gauvin Welland grew up on the St. Lawrence River and every Christmas Eve after midnight mass she enjoyed her mother's tourtière. She kept up the tradition of this French-Canadian wake-up celebration, réveillon, with her own children even when the family moved to England. She invited English friends to join them and after a while they, too, looked forward to the tradition. She remembers having great difficulty convincing her British butcher to grind the pork for the pies.

2 lb	minced pork	1 kg
1	large onion	1
1	small clove garlic	1
⅛ tsp	mace	0.5 mL
⅛ tsp	sage	0.5 mL
1	small potato	1
¼ cup	raisins	50 mL
	Salt and freshly ground pepper to taste	
	Boiling water	
	Pastry for double-crust 9-in (23-cm) pie	

Finely mince onion and garlic. Peel and grate potato. Place minced pork, onion, garlic, mace, sage, grated potato and raisins in large heavy-bottomed pot. Cover with boiling water, about 2 cups (500 mL). Cook, uncovered, over medium heat until meat is no longer pink and water is absorbed, 30 to 45 minutes. Stir frequently, reducing heat if necessary to avoid boiling. Remove from heat and set aside to cool. Skim off excess fat.

Preheat oven to 400°F (200°C). Meanwhile, prepare pastry. Line a pie plate with half the pastry. Prick with fork and bake 10 minutes. Cool to room temperature. Pour cooled meat mixture into pie shell. Cover with top crust. Crimp and seal edges and cut vents to allow steam to escape. Bake 10 minutes. Reduce heat to 350°F (180°C) and bake 30 more minutes until crust is light brown and filling is bubbly. Serve hot.

YIELD: 6 to 8 servings

Tourtière can be prepared days in advance and reheated. Cover with foil and bake at 350°F (180°C) for 20 minutes. If frozen, defrost in refrigerator before heating.

. . . .

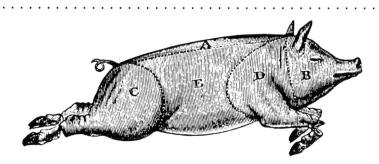

WILD RABBIT PIE

. . . .

In Boutilier's Point, Nova Scotia, little boys snare rabbits for stew. On Christmas Eve, Debbie Boutilier serves rabbit pie to her family. Her sister, mother and grandparents also prepare it every year. This pie is delicious enough to make it the main focus of Christmas Day, if you would like a change from turkey.

2	young rabbits, about 2 lb (1 kg)	2
2 tbsp	salt	25 mL
4	slices bacon	4
4	cloves garlic	4
1	onion	1
½ lb	mushrooms	250 g
¼ cup	butter	50 mL
1 cup	hot chicken stock OR hot water	250 mL
½ tsp	thyme	2 mL
	Salt and freshly ground pepper to taste	
	Short crust pastry for a double-crust 9-in (23-cm) pie	

Preheat oven to 350°F (180°C). Clean rabbits and cut each one into 9 pieces (4 leg, 2 rib, and 3 back). In large bowl, place rabbit, salt and enough cold water to cover. Refrigerate 3 or 4 hours or overnight. Drain rabbit pieces and pat dry. Dice bacon and fry in large skillet over medium-high heat until barely crisp. Remove bacon with a slotted spoon to two small or one large casserole dish. Sauté minced garlic and chopped onion in bacon fat until onion is translucent. Add sliced mushrooms and continue frying over medium heat, stirring until volume is reduced and mushrooms are slightly brown and crisp. Remove onions and mushrooms to casserole dish(es).

In large skillet, melt 2 tbsp (25 mL) butter. Fry rabbit on both sides over high heat and place in a large casserole. Spoon mushroom mixture over rabbit. Pour stock or water and thyme in skillet, scraping bottom to loosen all pan drippings. Pour over rabbit. Add salt and freshly ground pepper to taste. Cover and bake 1½ hours or more, until rabbit is tender. Add more liquid stock if necessary.

Remove casserole from oven to cool slightly. Roll out pie crust. Increase oven temperature to 425°F (220°C). Carefully place pastry on top of rabbit stew, sealing edges and cutting a steam vent. Return to oven long enough to brown crust and reheat filling, about 15 to 20 minutes.   **YIELD: 4 to 6 servings**

. . . .

BIGOS
(POLISH HUNTERS' STEW)

This very old traditional Polish dish calls for at least a half-pound of eight different kinds of meat, all braised individually. The recipe must have developed at a time when a hunter would come home every day with different game. It was fried up and added to the pot kept simmering at the back of the stove. The flavor improves with reheating, so it can be made a few days before you wish to serve it. Just make sure to refrigerate it properly.

1 lb	beef OR veal	500 g
1 lb	pork OR ham	500 g
½ lb	lamb	250 g
½ lb	venison OR rabbit	250 g
1 lb	chicken, duck, pheasant OR goose	500 g
4	carrots	4
4	celery ribs with leaves	4
6	onions	6
4	cloves garlic	4
	Fresh parsley	
8 cups	water OR meat broth	2 L
	Salt and freshly ground pepper to taste	
2-4 lb	sauerkraut	1-2 kg
1 lb	fresh mushrooms	500 g
6	strips bacon	6
½ lb	Polish sausage, sliced	250 g
1 tbsp	white sugar	15 mL
1-1½ cups	Madeira wine OR beer	250-375 mL

In a large skillet, brown each meat (except bacon and sausage) individually in bacon fat or vegetable oil. Place meats in a very large heavy-bottomed pot with lid. Add carrot, celery, 4 of the onions, garlic, parsley, broth, and salt and freshly ground pepper to taste. Cover and place over medium-low heat. Do not allow to boil. Cook until fork tender, at least 2 hours. Meanwhile, rinse and drain sauerkraut and place in another large pot over low heat. Add beer or wine and chopped sausage and simmer until meat in large pot is tender. Add more liquid if necessary. Remove meat from large pot. Strain cooking liquid and remove to large bowl. Chill and skim off most surface fat. Use vegetables for another purpose. Chop bacon and onions and sauté in large pot until onion is transparent. Add fresh mushrooms and continue cooking over medium heat until browned. Chop meat and add along with braising liquid, sugar, salt and pepper and sauerkraut mixture to large pot. Simmer uncovered for 30 to 45 minutes.   **YIELD: 6 qt (6 L)**

. . . .

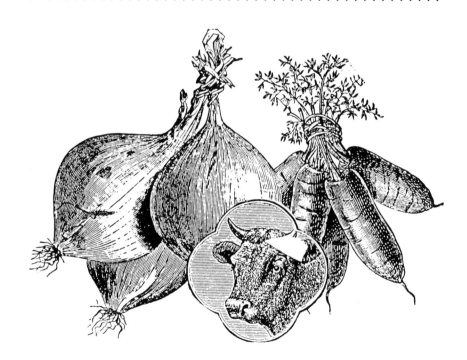

HOLUBSTI
(CABBAGE ROLLS)

Traditionally, Christmas Eve holubsti are meatless. You may wish to substitute additional rice for the meat and tomato juice for the beef broth. Adjust the sweet and sour taste to suit yourself.

1	large cabbage	1
¼ cup	butter	50 mL
1	onion	1
1 lb	lean ground beef	500 g
½ cup	white rice	125 mL
1 tsp	thyme AND/OR dried dillweed	5 mL
	Salt and freshly ground pepper to taste	
¼ tsp	allspice	1 mL
½ tsp	grated lemon rind	2 mL
3 cups	canned tomatoes, including liquid	750 mL
2 cups	sauerkraut, rinsed and drained	500 mL
2 cups	beef broth	500 mL
¼ cup	brown sugar	50 mL

Preheat oven to 325°F (160°C). Bring a very large kettle of water, half full, to a rolling boil. Core cabbage and place in kettle. Cover and cook until leaves are soft and can be easily peeled back. Remove cabbage to sink. Run cold water over cabbage and drain well. Carefully separate whole leaves. Set aside tough outer leaves. If inner cabbage is uncooked, place back in boiling water for a few more minutes. Meanwhile, prepare filling. Chop onion. In large skillet, melt butter and sauté onion and rice until onion is transparent. Crumble ground beef and add to skillet with rice, salt and pepper, thyme and dill, allspice and lemon rind, stirring often until meat is no longer pink. Set aside to cool.

Meanwhile, in a large bowl, combine tomatoes, sauerkraut, beef broth, brown sugar, salt and pepper. Coarsely chop whole tomatoes. Pour a ½-in (1-cm) layer of tomato mixture on bottom of deep-sided, greased 9 × 14-in (22.5 × 35-cm) pan.

To form cabbage rolls, place cabbage leaves on flat surface. Place ¼ cup (50 mL) filling at end of each leaf in a sausage shape. Roll over to cover filling with leaf. Tuck in sides and roll up. Place seam side down in pan. Top with remaining tomato mixture. Cover with outer cabbage leaves. Bake 2 hours or more, or all day in a lower temperature oven.

YIELD: about 15 cabbage rolls

. . . .

SWEET POTATOED PRUNES

A variation on candied yams (usually made with marsh-mallows!) this dish is easy to prepare in advance and reheat in oven, double boiler or microwave.

2	large sweet potatoes	2
10	prunes	10
¼ cup	apple juice	50 mL
1 tbsp	butter	15 mL
¼ tsp	cinnamon OR ginger	1 mL
⅓ cup	marmalade	75 mL
	Salt and freshly ground pepper to taste	

Preheat oven to 350°F (180°C). Peel and dice sweet potatoes and place in large buttered casserole dish. In small saucepan, place prunes and apple juice over medium-low heat. Cook, covered, until prunes are plumped and pits easily slip out. Remove and discard pits. Coarsely chop prunes and place back in apple juice liquid. Stir in cinnamon or ginger and marmalade and salt and freshly ground pepper to taste. Pour prune mixture over sweet potatoes. Cover with aluminum foil and bake about 35 minutes, until fork tender. Remove foil, stir and bake 5 minutes longer.   **YIELD: 4 to 6 small servings**

TRADITIONAL DESSERTS

It would be an understatement to say that dessert right after Christmas dinner is often unappreciated. I suppose some people are disciplined enough to leave room for dessert. But even with minuscule portions of turkey and trimmings, it all adds up to sensory overload.

We try to squeeze a few minutes or hours between the last bite of turkey and the first bite of plum pudding. If the climate allows, we drag the lethargic eaters out into the cold for some air. If not, we entice them into another room to try out a new game from under the tree. All the old-fashioned Christmas desserts — steamed puddings, mincemeat and trifle — are prepared well in advance of the big meal. Today we have the advantage of freezers, so a frozen dessert is just as, or more convenient. Here are some recipes you may want to turn into a family tradition.

ENGLISH TRIFLE

This is one of those dishes that actually tastes better after sitting overnight in the refrigerator. Layers of cake, custard, whipped cream, jam, fruit and sherry — yum. It is a grand thing to do with leftover cake when Christmas is over, too.

Custard

½ cup	white sugar	125 mL
¼ cup	cornstarch	50 mL
4	egg yolks	4
3 cups	milk	750 mL
1 tsp	vanilla	5 mL
1	9-in (23-cm) sponge OR pound cake	1
¼ cup	sherry	50 mL
¾ cup	strawberry jam	175 mL
2 cups	heavy cream	500 mL
1 cup	fresh or frozen strawberries	250 mL

In heavy-bottomed saucepan, combine sugar and cornstarch and whisk in egg yolks. Add milk and cook over medium-low heat, stirring constantly until thickened. Remove from heat and stir in vanilla. Set aside to cool.

To assemble: Cut cake into 8, ½-in (1-cm) thick slices. Place 4 slices on the bottom of a deep, non-metallic serving dish (preferably glass because the layers are pretty) with sides at least 5 in (12 cm) high. Sprinkle on half the sherry. Spread half the jam on cake. Whip 1 cup (250 mL) heavy cream until stiff and spread on cake. Carefully place remaining cake slices on cream layer. Sprinkle on remaining sherry and spread remaining jam. Top with custard. Cover with plastic wrap and refrigerate at least 4 hours but preferably overnight.

To serve: Slice or defrost strawberries. Whip remaining 1 cup (250 mL) cream until stiff. Serve individual portions with a dollop of whipped cream and a strawberry garnish.
YIELD: 8 to 10 servings

CHARLOTTE'S
FROZEN CREAM/CRUMB TORTE

Charlotte Reed's children are grown up but they still ask her to make this dessert for Christmas dinner. It can be made two or three weeks ahead of time and kept frozen until an hour before it is served. Use unsweetened frozen berries for best results.

1 cup	heavy cream	250 mL
½ cup	butter	125 mL
½ cup	icing sugar	125 mL
2	eggs	2
½ tsp	vanilla	2 mL
1 cup	finely crushed vanilla wafers	250 mL
1½ cups	crushed strawberries	375 mL
½ cup	finely chopped nuts	125 mL

In small bowl, whip cream until stiff and set aside. In another bowl, cream butter and sugar. Beat in eggs and vanilla. Butter large glass or ceramic pie plate or low-sided casserole. Pat ½ cup (125 mL) cookie crumbs on bottom of pie plate. Spread butter mixture evenly on crumbs. Top with strawberries. Fold nuts into whipped cream and spread on top of strawberry layer. Sprinkle on remaining cookie crumbs. Wrap well and freeze until ready to serve.   **YIELD: 8 to 10 servings**

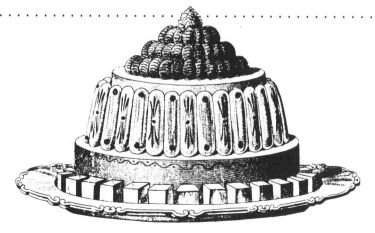

SWEET POTATO PIE

For a really smooth texture, purée the cooked sweet potato in a food mill, blender or food processor.

3	eggs	3
1 cup	brown sugar	250 mL
1¾ cups	cooked mashed sweet potato	425 mL
1¾ cups	milk	425 mL
¼ cup	melted butter	50 mL
¼ tsp	salt	1 mL
1 tsp	cinnamon	5 mL
1 tsp	nutmeg	5 mL
½ tsp	allspice	2 mL
	Pastry for a single-crust 9-in (23-cm) pie	

Preheat oven to 425°F (220°C). Roll out pastry, place in pie shell and crimp edges. Prick pastry with fork randomly in a few places so that it will not buckle while baking. Bake 5 minutes; remove from oven and set aside. Reduce oven heat to 350°F (180°C). Beat together all ingredients in large bowl. Pour into pie shell and bake 45 to 55 minutes, until crust is golden brown and center is firm.　**YIELD: 1 pie**

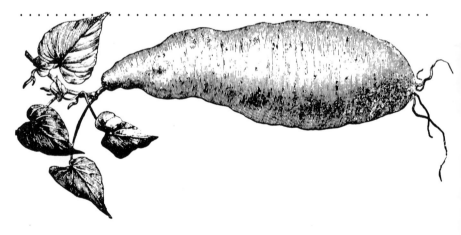

DANISH RICE PORRIDGE

This rice dish was originally an appetizer course served Christmas Eve in Denmark. It has evolved into a dessert, topped with their famous national liqueur.

3 cups	milk	750 mL
½ cup	white rice	125 mL
2 tbsp	butter	25 mL
¼ cup	white sugar	50 mL
1 tsp	vanilla	5 mL
½ cup	coarsely chopped blanched almonds	125 mL
1 cup	heavy cream	250 mL
¼ cup	cherry jam OR Cherry Herring	50 mL

In medium saucepan, place milk and rice over medium-high heat. Bring just to a boil. Cover, reduce heat and simmer 20 minutes. Add butter, sugar, vanilla and almonds. Set aside to cool to room temperature. In small bowl, beat cream until stiff. Gently fold whipped cream into rice mixture and pour into serving bowl. Chill until serving. Garnish with cherry jam or liqueur.   **YIELD: 4 to 6 servings**

PECAN PIE

. . . .

In the South, Christmas wouldn't be Christmas without pecan pie, sweet potato pie, or both. For a slight change from tradition, I add nutmeg and cinnamon.

3	eggs	3
1 cup	brown sugar	250 mL
⅓ cup	melted butter	75 mL
1 cup	dark corn syrup	250 mL
¼ tsp	salt	1 mL
1 tsp	vanilla	5 mL
¼ tsp	nutmeg	1 mL
¼ tsp	cinnamon	1 mL
1 cup	pecan halves	250 mL
	Pastry for a single-crust 9-in (23-cm) pie	

Preheat oven to 375°F (190°C). In large bowl, beat together eggs, brown sugar, butter, corn syrup, salt, vanilla, nutmeg and cinnamon. Roll out pastry, place in pie plate and crimp edges. Pour egg mixture into pie shell. Place pecans on top in swirl or any pattern. The top half will become toasted, giving the pecans more flavor than if stirred in. Bake 30 to 40 minutes until crust is golden brown and center is firm.   **YIELD: 1 pie**

. . . .

PECAN PIE *(see above)*

MINCE TARTS

. . . .

Mince tarts are pastry rounds cut out with a cookie cutter, filled with mincemeat and topped with another layer of pastry. They are sealed around the edges and baked on a cookie sheet. Making these fussy little things takes time and care. On a busy day, stick to the less finicky mince pie.

	Pastry for double-crust 9-in (23-cm) pie	
¾ cup	mincemeat	175 mL
1	egg for glaze	1

Preheat oven to 400°F (200°C). Roll half the pastry into a flat circle ¼ in (5 mm) thick. Cut with floured glass or cookie cutter into 8, 3-in (9-cm) rounds. Place circles on ungreased cookie sheets. In a cup, beat egg and use to dampen edges of pastry rounds. Place 1 rounded tbsp (15 mL) of mincemeat in the center of each round. Top with pastry round, and seal edges with flat side of fork. Brush beaten egg on pastry. Cut a few small vent holes; and bake 10 minutes. Reduce heat to 350°F (180°C) and bake 10 minutes more. Remove from oven and immediately remove tarts to cooling rack.   **YIELD: 8 tarts**

. . . .

MAKE TODAY, EAT TODAY MINCE PIE

· ·

Although aged mincemeat is more mellow, this pie is a good substitute in a pinch.

½ cup	orange juice	125 mL
1 cup	raisins	250 mL
½ cup	currants	125 mL
½ cup	candied peel	125 mL
½ tsp	nutmeg	2 mL
½ tsp	allspice OR cloves	2 mL
½ tsp	cinnamon	2 mL
½ tsp	grated lemon rind	2 mL
¼ cup	finely chopped beef suet	50 mL
1-2 cups	peeled, chopped apples	250-500 mL
½ cup	unsweetened applesauce	125 mL
¼ cup	brandy	50 mL
	Pastry for double-crust 9-in (23-cm) pie	

Preheat oven to 425°F (220°C). In a large enamel-coated saucepan, combine orange juice, raisins, currants, candied peel, and spices over medium heat. Bring to a boil. Reduce heat and simmer, covered, 15 minutes. Remove from heat and cool completely. Meanwhile, roll out bottom pastry crust and place it in pie plate. Stir lemon rind, suet, apples, applesauce and brandy into cooled raisin mixture. Pour into pie shell. Add a splash more brandy if desired. Roll out top crust and place on pie. Crimp edges and cut vent holes. Bake 10 minutes. Reduce heat to 350°F (180°C) and continue baking for 40 minutes. **YIELD: 1 pie**

· ·

AMBROSIA

. . . .

A favorite recipe in the South, it is sometimes served as a side dish.

1	fresh coconut	1
1	fresh pineapple	1
3	oranges	3
	Sugar to taste	

Pierce 3 eyes in coconut with large nail and hammer. Invert over glass to collect milk (reserve milk for other purposes). Gently tap coconut to crack shell. Pry out flesh. Cut off and discard brown skin with knife or potato peeler. Grate 2 cups (500 mL) of the meat and set aside. Cut off top and outside skin of pineapple. Discard woody core. Chop flesh into bite-size chunks. Peel oranges and slice into ¼-in (5-mm) rounds. Discard seeds. Layer grated coconut, pineapple chunks and orange rounds in serving dish. Sprinkle desired amount of sugar between layers. Cover and chill well before serving. **YIELD: 8 cups (2 L)**

. . . .

WASSAIL *(see page 200)*

CHAPTER 6

BOXING DAY & NEW YEAR'S

DRESSING UP THE LEFTOVERS

$\mathcal{I}$ have a friend who thinks turkey dinner is fine, but what he really looks forward to is turkey sandwiches on Boxing Day. He takes a homemade roll or two slices of fresh white bread, he slathers on mayonnaise and artfully places cooked turkey on one side. He tops this with a layer of leftover stuffing, a layer of cranberry sauce, a few peas if he can find them and bread. ⬛ Then there is the great Canadian culinary institution, the hot turkey sandwich. Cranberry sauce sets it off as does good old-fashioned ketchup. Zapped in the microwave, it is instant food. ⬛ My children practically cry with relief when they open up their sandwiches to find chunks of turkey, mayonnaise and lettuce, rather than peanut butter. ⬛ I don't know why leftovers get such bad press. I love them.

CHRISTMAS LEFTOVERS

Foods	Simple ideas
Turkey	*Hot turkey sandwiches *Turkey soup *Turkey salads Turkey salad sandwiches *Turkey biscuit pie *Chinese-style turkey fry
Ham	Ground ham and pickle sandwiches Potato and ham scallop Split pea soup Ham and cheese quiche
Roast beef	*Hot beef sandwich Beef fried rice Shepherd's pie
Mashed potatoes	Fried potato patties Topping for shepherd's pie
Cranberry sauce	*Cranberry apple crisp *Cranberry cake *Cranberry kysil
Mincemeat	*Mincemeat loaf
Bread	*Bread pudding French toast Croutons for salad Stuffing for future turkey
Wine	*Fruit compote
Cookies/Cakes	*Fruitcake crumble cheesecake Rice pudding
Eggnog	*Eggnog rice pudding
Cooked Vegetables: peas, beans, broccoli, cauliflower, carrots	Marinate in oil and vinegar dressing, chill and add to salad Add to soup broth Add to fried rice
Corn	*Corn fritters, corn chowder, corn bread
Winter squash	Squash pancakes Squash pie Squash or pumpkin bread

. . . .

*Recipes included in book

LEFTOVER TURKEY SOUP

If you are too tired to deal with the turkey bones on Christmas day, place them in a plastic bag and put them into the freezer until you are more in the mood. I sometimes make up the broth and put it outside overnight in the cold. The next day I finish the soup or place the broth in the freezer for a day when appetites are more enthusiastic.

1	turkey carcass	1
1	onion	1
1	carrot	1
1	rib celery	1
½ tsp	thyme OR dried dillweed	2 mL
½	bay leaf	½
	Fresh parsley	
	Salt and freshly ground pepper to taste	
	Cooked or chopped raw vegetables	
	Noodles, cooked	
	Rice OR leftover meat	

After meat and stuffing have been removed, break up turkey into quarters. In large pot, place the bones and whole onion, carrot, celery, dill, bay leaf and parsley, and water to cover. Place over high heat. Bring to a boil. Cover and simmer for 2 or more hours. While cooking, remove froth and scum and add more water if necessary. Submerge pot in sink of cold water. When cool, strain broth, discarding solids. Refrigerate. If you do not wish to use broth at this time, pour into heavy plastic bag, seal and freeze. An hour before you wish to eat soup, remove from refrigerator. Remove and discard some or all fat at top of soup. Place soup over medium heat and add any combination of cooked or chopped raw vegetables, noodles, cooked rice, leftover meat, salt and freshly ground pepper to taste. For most flavor, heat barely to warm through. Adjust seasonings. **YIELD: 6 to 10 servings**

CHINESE-STYLE TURKEY FRY

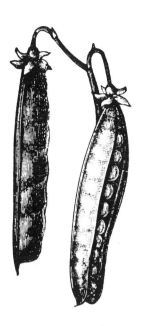

· ·

Take leftover turkey and gravy from Christmas dinner and transform them into something different. Serve on a bed of freshly steamed rice or heated up mashed potatoes.

2 tbsp	butter	25 mL
1	small onion, diced	1
1	garlic clove, minced	1
2 cups	sliced fresh mushrooms	500 mL
1½ cups	gravy OR turkey broth	375 mL
1 tbsp	soy sauce	15 mL
2 tbsp	honey	25 mL
½ tsp	ginger	2 mL
2 cups	sliced cooked turkey	500 mL
1 cup	raw or cooked peas OR green beans	250 mL

In large skillet, melt butter and sauté onion and garlic a few minutes until translucent. Add mushrooms and increase heat to medium. Fry until slightly browned. Add gravy or turkey broth, soy sauce, honey and ginger. Cook, stirring for a few minutes to allow flavors to combine. Add turkey and peas or beans and cook until heated through.   **YIELD: 4 servings**

· ·

HOT TURKEY OR
BEEF SANDWICH

. . . .

Homemade is way better than any restaurant version.

¼-½ cup	leftover gravy	50-125 mL
2	slices white bread OR	2
1	roll	1
½ cup	chopped or sliced leftover turkey	125 mL

In small saucepan, heat gravy over medium heat or in microwave until almost boiling. Place 1 slice of bread or bottom half of roll on serving plate. Top with turkey. Pour half of gravy over meat. Top with second slice of bread or top of roll. Top with remaining gravy. Serve with mashed potatoes, peas and ketchup or cranberry sauce.   **YIELD: 1 sandwich**

. . . .

FAMILY TURKEY SALAD

. . . .

Salad is a perfect antidote to Christmas overindulgence. This one is simple to prepare and the combinations of flavors and textures even appeal to children who don't like salad.

3 cups	chopped cooked turkey	750 mL
3	hard-cooked eggs	3
1	head iceberg lettuce	1
⅓ cup	chopped sweet pickles	75 mL
¼-½ cup	mayonnaise	50-125 mL
	Salt and freshly ground pepper to taste	

Cut lettuce into chunks and place in large salad bowl. Slice turkey and eggs and add. Add remaining ingredients. Toss and serve immediately.   **YIELD: 4 servings**

. . . .

LIGHT TURKEY SALAD

Marinating the cooked turkey for a few minutes perks up the flavor and texture.

¼ cup	quality olive oil	50 mL
2 tbsp	herb vinegar	25 mL
3 cups	cold cooked turkey	750 mL
1	red OR yellow pepper	1
1	head romaine lettuce OR any greens	1
1	carrot, cut into thin coins	1
¼ cup	grated or cubed cheese (optional)	50 mL
	Salt and freshly ground pepper to taste	

In large salad bowl, combine olive oil and herb vinegar. Add turkey and coat. Allow to marinate for 5 minutes before tossing in remaining ingredients: rings of pepper, torn lettuce, carrot, cheese and salt and pepper. For an easy meal, serve with hot buttered toast.   **YIELD: 4 small servings**

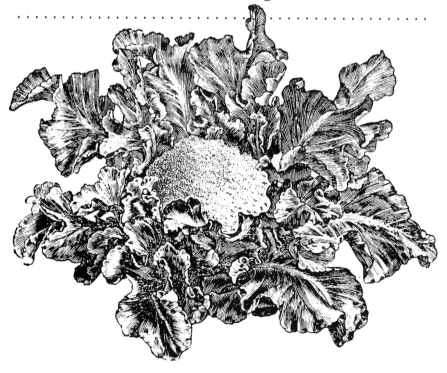

TURKEY BISCUIT PIE

4 cups	cooked turkey chunks	1 L
3	potatoes, peeled and cubed	3
2	onions, peeled and quartered	2
2	carrots, peeled and sliced	2
½ cup	fresh or frozen peas	125 mL
⅓ cup	butter	75 mL
¼ cup	white flour	50 mL
2-2½ cups	turkey liquid: pan juices, soup OR gravy	500-625 mL
1 cup	cream OR milk	250 mL
	Salt and freshly ground pepper to taste	
	Pinch of tarragon OR dillweed	

Biscuits

2 cups	white flour	500 mL
1½ tbsp	baking powder	20 mL
¼ tsp	salt	1 mL
1 tbsp	white sugar	15 mL
⅓ cup	shortening	75 mL
¾ cup	milk	175 mL

When making Turkey Biscuit Pie, substitute vegetables of your choice such as broccoli, turnip, cauliflower, beans, squash. Roll out the biscuits on floured waxed paper, for easier cleanup.

Preheat oven to 450°F (230°C). Place turkey in large casserole or 2 small pie plates. Cook potatoes, onions and carrots until half cooked through by steaming over hot water or in microwave. Place vegetables in casserole. Add peas. In medium saucepan, melt butter and stir in flour. Cook, stirring constantly, for 2 or 3 minutes. Add turkey liquid and cream or milk, salt and pepper, tarragon or dillweed, and continue cooking and stirring until slightly thickened. Pour over turkey and vegetables. Into medium bowl, sift flour, baking powder, salt and sugar. Rub in shortening until it resembles coarse meal. Stir in milk. Pat it, turn it over and pat it again just enough times to hold it together. Roll out to ¾ in (2 cm) on floured surface. Cut into squares or circles. Place biscuits on warm turkey mixture and bake about 15 minutes, until biscuits are light brown and mixture is bubbly.   **YIELD: 4 to 6 servings**

TURKEY BISCUIT PIE
(see above)

MINCEMEAT LOAF

This fruity, spicy quick bread is basically a biscuit with mincemeat stirred in at the end. It has an old-fashioned coffee cake taste.

2 cups	white flour	500 mL
⅓ cup	white sugar	75 mL
2 tsp	baking powder	10 mL
⅓ cup	butter	75 mL
1	egg	1
¾-1 cup	milk	175-250 mL
1¼ cups	mincemeat	300 mL

Glaze

½ cup	icing sugar	125 mL
1 tsp	vanilla	5 mL
1 tbsp	water	15 mL

Preheat oven to 375°F (190°C). Into large bowl, sift flour, sugar and baking powder. Cut in butter until mixture resembles coarse meal. In small bowl, blend together egg, smaller amount of milk and mincemeat. Stir egg mixture into flour mixture just until moistened. Add more milk to make slightly lumpy, runny batter. The moisture content of mincemeat varies, so the amount of milk required also varies. Pour into small buttered loaf pan and bake 40 to 50 minutes, until brown. Remove from oven, allow to cool a minute and turn out onto cooling rack. Meanwhile, combine icing sugar, vanilla and water to form a paste. Place loaf on serving plate and drizzle glaze over warm loaf. Serve warm or cold.   **YIELD: 1 small loaf**

CRANBERRY CAKE

½ cup	butter	125 mL
¾ cup	white sugar	175 mL
2	eggs	2
2 cups	white flour	500 mL
1 tsp	baking powder	5 mL
1 tsp	baking soda	5 mL
1 cup	yogurt	250 mL
1 tsp	vanilla OR almond extract	5 mL
2 cups	cranberry sauce	500 mL

Glaze

1 cup	icing sugar	250 mL
1 tsp	vanilla	5 mL
1-1½ tbsp	milk	15-20 mL
½ cup	finely chopped walnuts	125 mL
	Fresh cranberries for garnish	

Preheat oven to 350°F (180°C). In large bowl, cream butter and beat in sugar and eggs. Into medium bowl, sift flour, baking powder and baking soda. Add flour mixture to butter mixture alternately with yogurt. Stir in vanilla or almond extract. Pour half the batter into greased and floured bundt pan. Add 1 cup (250 mL) layer of cranberry sauce. Top with remaining batter and then cranberry sauce. Bake 55 minutes or until a toothpick comes out dry and crumb-free. Meanwhile, in a small bowl, blend icing sugar, vanilla and milk until smooth. Remove cake from oven. Allow to rest 10 minutes and invert on a cooling rack. Drizzle on frosting. Sprinkle on walnuts and cranberries.
YIELD: 1 cake

CRANBERRY APPLE CRISP

A variation on our family standby, the cranberries give it a rosy hue and a tart cherry-like flavor.

3-4 cups	peeled, coarsely chopped apples	750 mL-1 L
1 cup	cranberry sauce	250 mL

Topping

1 cup	white flour	250 mL
1 cup	old-fashioned rolled oats	250 mL
1 cup	brown sugar	250 mL
1 tsp	cinnamon OR allspice	5 mL
½ cup	butter	125 mL

Preheat oven to 350°F (180°C). In buttered, 8-in (20-cm) square deep glass dish or casserole, combine apples and cranberry sauce. In medium bowl, blend flour, oats, brown sugar and cinnamon or allspice. Rub in butter until mixture resembles coarse meal. Sprinkle flour mixture on top of apple mixture. Bake 30 minutes, until slightly browned and bubbly. Serve with ice cream or heavy cream.   **YIELD: 8 servings**

CRANBERRY KYSIL

This simple Eastern European dessert, made of cooked or stewed fruit, is thickened with cornstarch. Leftover cranberry sauce can be easily transformed into delicious kysil.

2 cups	cranberry sauce	500 mL
1 cup	orange OR cranberry juice	250 mL
½ tsp	grated orange rind	2 mL
1 tbsp	freshly squeezed lemon juice	15 mL
1-2 tbsp	cornstarch	15-25 mL
1 cup	heavy cream	250 mL

In medium stainless or enamel-coated saucepan, combine cranberry sauce, ¾ cup (175 mL) juice, orange rind and lemon juice over medium heat. Bring to a boil and reduce to low. In a cup, whisk together cornstarch and remaining juice until smooth. Stir cornstarch mixture into cranberry mixture, stirring often until thickened and smooth. Pour into 1 large or 4 small serving dishes. Cool to room temperature and refrigerate. Serve with heavy cream.   **YIELD: 4 servings**

FRUITCAKE CRUMBLE CHEESECAKE

1 lb	cream cheese	500 g
1 tsp	freshly squeezed lemon juice	5 mL
2	eggs	2
⅓ cup	white sugar	75 mL
2½ cups	crumbled fruitcake AND/OR cookies	625 mL

Preheat oven to 325°F (160°C). Chop fruitcake and/or cookies to a coarse consistency by hand or in a food processor. Into bottom of a buttered 8-in (20-cm) square cake pan, press 2 cups (500 mL) crumbs. Beat together cream cheese, lemon juice, eggs and sugar in food processor, with electric mixer, or by hand. Pour cream cheese mixture onto fruitcake crumbs. Sprinkle on remaining fruitcake crumbs. Bake 30 to 35 minutes until corners puff. Remove from oven, allow to reach room temperature. Chill well before serving. Store in refrigerator.
YIELD: 64, 1-in (2.5-cm) servings

EGGNOG RICE PUDDING

2	eggs	2
1½ cups	eggnog	375 mL
¼ cup	raisins	50 mL
½ cup	milk	125 mL
2 cups	cooked rice	500 mL
¼ cup	cookie OR cake crumbs	50 mL

Preheat oven to 325°F (160°C). Beat eggs and eggnog. In medium bowl, add raisins, milk and rice. Pour into buttered 1½-qt (1.5-L) glass baking pan or casserole. Top with crumbs. Bake 45 minutes or more, until firm and a knife inserted in middle will come out clean.   **YIELD: 8 servings**

SOME NEW YEAR'S FOOD TRADITIONS

In European countries such as Scotland and Holland which were influenced by Calvinism, Christmas is a low-key holiday. They make up for it with big New Year's celebrations. But in North America, while the odd superstition lingers, the New Year's holiday is tradition in the making.

I like the fact that New Year's is a day we can celebrate differently every year, in our own personal way. As a child it was a treat to stay up late; to munch on potato chips and drink pop and watch the New Year come in on television. As a teenager it was a thrill to do the same thing in a room full of rambunctious friends, anxiously awaiting midnight to kiss someone I was too shy to even speak to the rest of the year.

As an adult on New Year's Eve I have hosted blowout-style parties and quiet dinners, eaten at Chinese restaurants and

taken long walks on the beach watching the North Atlantic in the moonlight. I also remember a few years when my spouse and I were so self-content, or just tired out, that we went to bed at 10 p.m.

After the anticlimax of Christmas, the New Year's holiday lets us down easily by giving us something else to look forward to. It is a mark in time set aside for us to reflect on the past, and to set our sights on brighter things for the future. Best of all, we can celebrate it any way we like. I relish this day.

Wassail Song

Here we come a-wassailing
Among the leaves so green.
Here we come a-wandering
So fair to be seen:

Love and joy come to you
And to you your wassail too,
And God bless you,
  and send you
A happy New Year,
And God send you
A happy New Year.

—Anonymous

WASSAIL

An early Anglo-Saxon toast, "Waes-hail," means "Be whole!" The response is "Drink-hail," or "Good Health!" The toasting beverage is also called wassail. Decorate your wassail bowl with ribbons and evergreens and fill it with hot spiced ale and cooked apples. It is usually served on Twelfth Night (Epiphany) or on New Year's Eve or New Year's Day when wassail processions go from house to house. Sometimes the bands of neighbors wander into the orchards and sprinkle the apple trees, grateful for the past harvest and toasting a fruitful year to come.

6	apples	6
6 tbsp	brown sugar	90 mL
6 cups	beer OR ale	1.5 L
½ tsp	ginger	2 mL
½ tsp	cinnamon	2 mL
½ tsp	grated nutmeg	2 mL

Preheat oven to 350°F (180°C). Core but do not peel apples. Fill each with 1 tbsp (15 mL) brown sugar. Place in buttered baking pan and bake about 30 minutes, until fork tender. In large saucepan, place beer and spices over medium heat. Bring just to a boil. Place apples in decorated serving bowl. Gently pour in beer. **YIELD: 6 to 8 servings**

SCOTTISH BLACK BUN

Jean Watt's Scottish father was a master baker who used a yeast dough to wrap the fruit filling of Black Bun. It is made for Hogmanay, the Scottish New Year. Use the Basic Sweet Bread Dough recipe in Chapter 4.

3 cups	raisins	750 mL
3 cups	currants	750 mL
1 cup	rum OR brandy	250 mL
2 cups	candied lemon and orange peel	500 mL
½ cup	chopped blanched almonds	125 mL
1 tsp	cinnamon	5 mL
1 tsp	ground coriander	5 mL
½ tsp	nutmeg	2 mL
½ tsp	ginger	2 mL
¼ tsp	white pepper	1 mL
1	recipe Basic Sweet Bread (page 133)	1

In medium bowl, combine raisins, currants and rum or brandy. Set aside to let fruit plump up. Drain fruit (you can save and drink the liquid) and place in large bowl with remaining ingredients. Preheat oven to 350°F (180°C). Follow instructions for Basic Sweet Bread Dough. After it has doubled in bulk, punch it down and divide into 3 even pieces. Take 2 of the pieces and roll them into flat circles about ½ in (1 cm) thick and 10 in (25 cm) in diameter. Take the remaining piece. Cut it in half and knead it into 2 balls. Set balls aside, covered. Place half the filling on each flat circle. With a pulling up of the edges and pushing down movement, knead the filling into the dough. Poke back fruit that separates. Knead until fully combined into neat balls. Set aside. Roll out remaining dough balls on lightly floured surface into flat circles about ¼ in (5 mm) thick and 10 in (25 cm) across. Place filled dough balls in center of flat circles. Wrap and seal filling with flat circle by pulling up edges. Pleat dough to take up excess, and pinch edges closed. Place seam side down in buttered, deep stainless or ceramic ovenproof bowl, about 8 in (20 cm) in diameter and 4 in (10 cm) deep. Pierce top with a long needle to allow steam to escape. Bake 1 to 1½ hours. **YIELD: 2 round loaves**

HOPPING JOHN

Hot baked ham, biscuits and Hopping John is the New Year's Day dinner that Mary Lucia Blacksher remembers eating as a child in Charleston, South Carolina.

We have substituted bacon for the usual salt pork. A ham bone may also be cooked along with the peas to impart a salty pork flavor. Use either the crushed chili (for a hot dish) or the black pepper (for a cooler one). Do not use both!

1 cup	dried black-eyed peas	250 mL
½ tsp	crushed red chili OR freshly ground black pepper to taste	2 mL
4	strips bacon	4
1	onion	1
	Salt to taste	
1 cup	white rice	250 mL

To clean, place peas in large sieve and wash by running cold tap water through. In a large pot, soak peas overnight by covering with about 8 cups (2 L) water. Discard any peas that float. Next day, drain peas and place them with 5 to 6 cups (1.25 to 1.5 L) water, chili or black pepper and salt in a large pot. Bring to boil, cover and simmer until tender, about 1 hour. Add more water if necessary to prevent sticking. Finely chop bacon and onion. In large skillet, fry bacon over medium heat until half cooked through. Add onion and cook until soft. When peas are tender, add bacon, onion, rice and 2 cups (500 mL) water to beans. Bring to a boil, cover and simmer until rice is soft, about 20 minutes. **YIELD: 6 servings**

LINDA JANE'S LUCKY DIME
BLACK-EYED PEAS

· ·

Linda Jane Mueller and her neighbors in Dallas, Texas, eat black-eyed peas and corn bread just after midnight on New Year's Eve. They put a few dimes in with the peas and whoever gets one will have good luck in the upcoming year. The cook scratches one of the dimes and if he or she gets that particular coin, it means a year of financial good fortune. Linda Jane swears that it worked for her last year. She found $50 lying in the street. In other parts of the South, black-eyed peas and collards are served in restaurants and homes New Year's Day. The peas are for good luck with pocket change, the collards bring luck in acquiring green folding money.

1 cup	dried black-eyed peas	250 mL
1	onion, finely chopped	1
1 tsp	seeded jalapeño pepper OR Freshly ground black pepper to taste	5 mL
	Salt to taste	
	Dimes	

To clean, place peas in large sieve and wash by running cold tap water through. In a large pot, soak peas overnight by covering with about 8 cups (2 L) water. Discard any peas that float. Next day, drain peas and place them with 5 to 6 cups (1.25 to 1.5 L) water, onion, seeded jalapeño pepper or freshly ground black pepper and salt to taste in large pot. Bring to boil, cover, and simmer until tender, about 1 hour. Add more water if necessary to prevent sticking. Scrub dimes in hot soapy water. Rinse well and stir into peas just before serving.   **YIELD: 4 cups (1 L)**

· ·

OLIEBOLLEN

. . . .

Leni Seinen grew up in Ijmyden in the Netherlands and immigrated to Canada after the war. She vividly remembers New Year's Day when her mother would fry up a big batch of these apple currant fritters. So did most of her neighbors, because she remembers that when they attended the New Year's Day service, the church was filled with the fragrance of oil-fried oliebollen.

1 tsp	white sugar	5 mL
¼ cup	hot water	50 mL
1 tbsp	dried yeast	15 mL
1	OR package dried yeast	1
¼ cup	white sugar	50 mL
1 cup	warm milk	250 mL
1	egg	1
1 tsp	vanilla	2 mL
2½ cups	white flour	625 mL
½ tsp	salt	2 mL
1	apple	1
½ cup	currants	125 mL
	Oil for deep frying	
1 cup	icing sugar	250 mL

In a cup, dissolve 1 tsp (5 mL) sugar in water and stir in yeast. Set aside in warm spot for 10 minutes to allow yeast to soften and bubble up. In large bowl, combine milk, remaining sugar, yeast mixture, egg and vanilla. Peel, core and finely dice apple. Sift together flour and salt and stir into milk mixture along with currants and diced apple. Do not knead. Cover and allow to rise until double in bulk. Place vegetable oil in heavy-bottomed saucepan or deep fat fryer and heat oil to 375°F (190°C). Drop 1 tbsp (15 mL) of dough at a time in hot fat. Fry a few at a time until golden (about 5 minutes). Do not crowd or oil temperature will drop and oliebollen will absorb grease. Turn over halfway through cooking. Remove to absorbent paper towelling. Place icing sugar in paper bag. Toss hot oliebollen in bag, to coat with icing sugar. Repeat until all dough is used up. **YIELD: 2 dozen**

. . . .

OLIEBOLLEN *(see above)*

HOT CORN BREAD

Serve this corn bread with Hopping John or black-eyed peas. While seeding and mincing jalapeño peppers, use rubber gloves and do not touch nose, eyes or mouth. The seeds are extremely irritating. Crushed dry chilis or tabasco sauce are easily substituted.

½ cup	white flour	125 mL
1 tbsp	white sugar	15 mL
½ tsp	salt	2 mL
1 tbsp	baking powder	15 mL
1 cup	white OR yellow cornmeal	250 mL
1	egg	1
1 cup	milk	250 mL
2 tbsp	melted butter OR bacon fat OR vegetable oil	25 mL
1 cup	frozen defrosted whole corn kernels	250 mL
2 tsp	seeded jalapeño pepper OR	10 mL
1 tbsp	crushed dry chili pepper OR	15 mL
2 tsp	tabasco sauce	10 mL

Preheat oven to 400°F (200°C). Into medium bowl, sift together flour, sugar, salt and baking powder. Stir in cornmeal. In a small bowl, whisk together egg, milk and melted butter or bacon fat or vegetable oil. Stir in corn and jalapeño pepper, chili pepper or tabasco sauce. Generously grease an 8-in (20-cm) square baking pan with butter, bacon fat or vegetable oil. Place in oven. Beat egg and milk mixtures just until smooth. Carefully remove hot pan from oven. Pour corn bread dough in pan and bake 20 to 30 minutes until light brown. Cut into squares and serve warm. **YIELD: 1 cake**

Index